THE MAKING
OF *Jonathan Wild*

—

BY WILLIAM ROBERT IRWIN

THE MAKING
OF *Jonathan Wild*

A STUDY IN THE LITERARY METHOD

OF HENRY FIELDING

ARCHON BOOKS
HAMDEN, CONNECTICUT
1966

ORIGINALLY PUBLISHED AS
NUMBER 153 OF THE COLUMBIA
UNIVERSITY STUDIES IN ENGLISH
AND COMPARATIVE LITERATURE

LIBRARY OF CONGRESS CATALOG CARD NUMBER: 66-12324
PRINTED IN THE UNITED STATES OF AMERICA

TO MY MOTHER AND FATHER

Preface

IN CONTRAST with his masterpieces *Joseph Andrews* and *Tom Jones, Jonathan Wild* is one of Henry Fielding's minor works; but as a study in the literary method of a great novelist it merits the full critical analysis which it has not previously been accorded. An understanding of this work depends upon the answers to two questions: What material for the writing of *Jonathan Wild* was available to Fielding? How did he use, enlarge, and shape this material to the fulfillment of his purpose? The synthesis of already existing data—biographical and historical, ethical, and literary— and actual creation which produced *Jonathan Wild*, constitute a process best summarized by the word "making." Hence the present title.

I have not attempted to discover the "sources" of *Jonathan Wild*, for the reason that Fielding drew his matter not so much from specific books as from historical, ethical, and literary traditions. Nor have I been concerned with analyzing the spiritual and emotional part of the creative process as it must have taken place in Fielding's mind while he wrote *Jonathan Wild*. Available evidence provides no tools for such deep searching. The nature of this subject demanded also that the discussion of "greatness" and "goodness" as concepts in the literature of popular morality be limited to the moral background of Fielding's own time, although these concepts have received wide and varied expression in the literature of all countries and all ages. I hope in a future study to give the literary expression of this aspect of the history of popular ethics the attention which it deserves.

Of my many debts of gratitude there are several which I wish particularly to acknowledge. The officers of the Yale University Library granted me the freedom of the excellent Fielding Collection. Professor George Sherburn of Harvard University and Professor Hoxie Neale Fairchild of Hunter College supervised this work in its early stages and contributed much to its formation. Professors Marjorie H. Nicolson, Oscar James Campbell, and Ernest Hunter Wright, all of Columbia University, have spared no effort in giving direction, criticism, and encouragement. The generous assistance of my wife has been unfailing and invaluable.

Finally, acknowledgments are due to the following for permission to quote copyrighted material: George Bell and Sons, Ltd.; The Clarendon Press, Oxford; Constable and Co., Ltd.; J. M. Dent and Sons, Ltd.; the editors of *English Literary History;* Houghton Mifflin Co.; Librairie Hachette; William Hodge and Co., Ltd.; Michael Joseph, Ltd.; the editors of the *Journal of English and Germanic Philology* and the University of Illinois Press; The Modern Language Association of America; the editors of *Philological Quarterly;* George Routledge and Sons, Ltd.; and La Société des Belles Lettres.

WILLIAM ROBERT IRWIN

New York
June 7, 1941

Contents

THE MAKING

OF *Jonathan Wild*

CHAPTER ONE

BIOGRAPHICAL AND HISTORICAL

BACKGROUND

THE LONG satirical moral narrative, *The Life of Mr. Jonathan Wild the Great,* which fills the third volume of *Miscellanies by Henry Fielding, Esq.,* is based in part on the complex of facts and traditions concerning Jonathan Wild, the notorious receiver, thief, and thief-taker who was hanged at Tyburn in 1725. During the final years of his life Jonathan Wild became an object of almost universal contempt and hatred. Soon after his death, political satirists associated with the Opposition to Sir Robert Walpole saw the effectiveness of comparing the methods employed by Jonathan Wild and by the Prime Minister whom they sought to defame. Frequent use of this device resulted in the obscuration of biographical details concerning Jonathan Wild and in the general acceptance of a highly simplified conception of his character, in which recollection of the man himself had little part.

Fielding doubtless knew the facts about the life of Jonathan Wild. He was far more interested, however, in the great rogue's reputation, both before and after his death, and in the connotation which the political writers had attached to his name. In fact, Jonathan Wild the man meant far less to Fielding than did Jonathan Wild the symbol. Consequently, in writing *Jonathan Wild* Fielding made use of only a small part of the biographical material which was available—adopted almost unchanged the conventional characterization of his central figure—and added a number of characters and incidents of his own invention. Essential to an understanding of the making of Fielding's *Jonathan Wild,* therefore, is an analysis of the background of facts and traditions concerning Jonathan Wild himself, against which this work was projected.

JONATHAN WILD THE MAN

Very few facts about Jonathan Wild's early life and criminal activities are known. It is reasonably certain that he was born in Wolverhampton, Staffordshire, in 1683, of poor and respectable parents. After a very brief time at the village Free School, he was apprenticed to a buckle-maker, but apparently prosecution for a youthful crime caused him, about 1700, to desert his master and his first wife, Amy, and leave his birthplace. He seems to have gone directly to London and soon after arrival to have been arrested, either for debt or vagrancy, and imprisoned in the Wood Street Compter. Here he spent the next four or five years. During this period he met and married a pickpocket and prostitute named Mary Milliner, and under her tutelage began within the prison itself a career of petty crime and extortion. This occupation was profitable, particularly after he was made assistant turnkey and given the freedom of the prison. Mary Milliner and Jonathan Wild continued their professional alliance after being released, merely shifting their center of operations from the Compter to a bawdyhouse in Lewkenor Lane. In 1708 Wild abandoned the dangerous business of ordinary thievery to become a receiver, a thief-taker, and the director of a gang of assorted criminals.[1] To this triple occupation he devoted himself until he was hanged in 1725.

For some years after setting up as thief-taker Wild apparently achieved no particular fame. His name does not appear in connection with the capture of any of the criminals memorialized in *A Complete History of the Lives and Robberies of the Most Notorious Highwaymen, Footpads, Shoplifts, and Cheats of Both Sexes*, written in 1714 by Captain Alexander Smith, a scribbler who had a thorough knowledge of the London underworld. In 1716, according to the statement of his hireling author, Wild received general applause for his part in apprehending the murderers of a certain Mrs. Knapp.[2] Such an assertion, particularly when unsupported by any other mention of the case, is not trustworthy. Withal, it is likely that after becoming a thief-taker and receiver Wild passed about ten years in busy obscurity, working out the system of organized crime which until 1725 resisted both law and public opinion and made Jonathan Wild himself a "common Theme of Conversation."[3]

To maintain his good name Wild, about 1718, "caused himself to be proclaimed, in the *Weekly Journal,* Thief-Catcher General of *Great Britain* and *Ireland,*"[4] began carrying a staff as a symbol of his authority,[5] and moved into pretentious quarters near the Old Bailey.[6] For a time, indeed, he was regarded by many as an honest and useful citizen. His office became the first place of inquiry for any missing property thought to have been stolen.[7] The property was always retrieved and Jonathan Wild never failed to receive "gifts," both from the owner and from the thief. Those in charge of administering the ineffectual machinery of justice were so grateful to Wild for apprehending and providing evidence against criminals that they ignored the obvious illegality of his business.[8] Indeed, Defoe felt justified in writing: "He acquired a strange and indeed unusual reputation for a mighty honest man, till his success hardened him to put on a face of public service on it. . . ."[9]

The best summary of Wild's ruthlessly administered system of organized crime is contained in the eleven "Informations" lodged against him at the time of his trial. As reported in *The Political State of Great Britain,* the "Informations" were as follows:

I. That he had for many Years past, been a Confederate with great Numbers of Highwaymen, Pick-pockets, House-breakers &c.

II. That he had form'd a kind of Corporation of Thieves, of which he was the Director; and that his pretended Services in detecting and prosecuting Offenders, consisted only in bringing those to the Gallows who concealed their Booty or refused to share it with him.

III. That he had divided the Town and Country into Districts, and appointed distinct Gangs for each, who regularly accounted with him for their Robberies. He had also a particular Set to steal at Churches in time of Divine Service; and also other moving Detachments to attend at Court on Birth-Days, Balls, &c. and upon both Houses of Parliament, Circuits and County Fairs.

IV. That the Person's employ'd by him were for the most part Felons convict, who have returned from Transportation before their due Time was expired; of whom he made Choice for his Agents because they could not be legal evidence against him, and because he had it in his own Power to take from them what Part of the Stolen Goods he pleased, and otherwise abuse, or even Hang them, at his Will and Pleasure.

V. That he had from time to time supplied such convicted Felons with Money and Cloaths, and lodged them in his own House, the better to conceal them; particularly some against whom there are now Informations for diminishing and counterfeiting Broad-Pieces and Guineas.

VI. That he had not only been a Receiver of Stolen Goods as well as of Writings of all Kinds for near 15 Years, last past, but frequently been a Confederate, and robb'd along with the above mentioned convicted Felons.

VII. That in order to carry on these vile Practices, and to gain some Credit with the ignorant Multitude, he usually carried about him a short Silver Staff, as a Badge of Authority from the Government, which he used to produce when he himself was concerned in robbing.

VIII. That he had under his Care and Direction several Warehouses for receiving and concealing Stolen Goods, and also a Ship for carrying off Jewels, Watches, and other valuable Goods to *Holland,* where he had a superannuated thief for his factor.[10]

IX. That he kept in Pay several Artists to make Alterations, and transform Watches, Seals, Snuff Boxes, Rings, and other valuable Things that they might not be known, several of which he used to present to such Persons as he thought might be of service to him.

X. That he seldom help'd the Owners to lost Notes & Papers, unless he found them able to specify and describe them exactly, and then insisted on more than half the Value.

XI. That he had frequently sold humane Blood, by procuring false Evidence to swear Persons into Facts of which they were not Guilty; sometimes to prevent them from being evidences against himself, at other Times for the Sake of the Great Reward given by the Government.[11]

Popular resentment against this infamous system and its creator, Jonathan Wild, began as soon as he came into prominence. In fact, Parliament in 1718 passed a law, probably directed at Wild, making it a crime to receive rewards for the return of stolen goods.[12] Wild evaded this by receiving only "gifts" from the owner and from the thief.[13] Contemporary accounts indicate that neither Parliament nor public opinion forced Wild to curtail his activities.[14] The newspapers of the time frequently printed advertisements like the following:

Stolen out of the Shop of Mr. John Chiswell, at Lutterworth in Leicestershire, the following Goods: [Here a list is given.] If any Person concern'd in the said Robbery will discover his Accomplices, so that they be brought to Justice, to Mess. Thomas and Alexander Dyer, Linnen-Drapers, at the Blue Anchor, Stocks-Market, or to Mr. Jonathan Wild, in the Old Bailey, he shall have *Ten* Guineas Reward.[15]

Even more common are accounts of Wild's captures of suspected felons, who were, to be sure, usually members of a rival gang or rebels from his own organization. The following notice is typical:

Of the three Men lately apprehended by Mr. *Jonathan Wild,* for a Robbery committed lately in *Leicester-Fields* upon Mr. *Wasey,* a Surgeon, one is committed to Newgate, another to the Marshalsea, and the third, who hath made considerable Discoveries, and is to be Evidence against his Accomplices, is secured in the Compter.[16]

Apprehending criminals was a profitable activity. Wild received £40 for each one who was eventually hanged,[17] besides incalculable returns from the loyalty which each hanging inspired in the members of his gang.

Such ruthlessness, although immediately remunerative, hastened Jonathan Wild's ruin and death. The people of London might have submitted almost indefinitely to his system of plundering them, but they would not tolerate his traffic in human lives. Resentment on this score was brought to a climax by Wild's part in the apprehension and hanging of two celebrated criminals—Joseph Blake, alias Blueskin, and Jack Sheppard.

Blueskin was a highwayman and housebreaker, at one time associated with Wild's gang. Because of disagreements over the disposal of booty Blueskin rebelled, and with some desperate companions established an independent organization which specialized in robbery and murder.[18] Wild persecuted Blueskin indefatigably,[19] and on October 2, 1724, captured him.[20] He was forthwith committed to Newgate, charged with a capital offense, speedily tried, condemned, and sentenced.[21] After sentence had been passed, Jonathan Wild visited him in Newgate. According to the account in *The British Journal*:

Mr. Wild being there drinking a Glass of Wine with him [Blueskin], he said to Mr. *Wild,* "You may put in a Word for me as well as for another Person." To which Mr. *Wild* replied, "I cannot do it, you are certainly a dead Man." Whereupon *Blake* on a sudden seized Wild by the Neck, and with a little Clasp-Knife cut his Throat in a very dangerous Manner...."[22]

Although the story of Blueskin was widely circulated, Wild's protracted persecution and final capture of Jack Sheppard excited the town still more and completed the ruin of Wild's already damaged reputation. Sheppard was a housebreaker who refused to come under Wild's government.[23] Sometime in July, 1724, Wild took him up and placed him in New Prison. He promptly escaped, and was promptly retaken by Jonathan Wild.[24] With this debut Sheppard began a career of prison-breaking. He made four more escapes, the last one of which involved breaking through half a dozen barred doors and walls surrounding the Castle Room of Newgate. Five times Jonathan Wild personally recaptured him.

As his escapes multiplied, popular opinion quickly made Sheppard into something of an outlaw hero. Defoe's reports of his activities appear frequently in *Applebee's Journal* from August through November, 1724. On November 7 Jonathan Wild recaptured Sheppard for the last time. A week later, having been convicted partially on evidence given by Wild himself, he was sentenced to be hanged. Public excitement rose during his final confinement. Sheppard was visited in the Condemned Hold by several famous persons,[25] among them Sir James Thornhill, who painted two portraits of him.[26] Many others were willing to pay for a sight of him.[27] It seems that several clergymen "preached the adventures of Jack Sheppard," using him as an example of the folly of striving to preserve the flesh.[28] Defoe records the following note about the period before Sheppard was hanged: "In short, it was a week of the greatest noise and idleness among mechanics that has been known in London; and Parker and Pettis, two lyrics, subsisted many days comfortably upon ballads and letters about Sheppard."[29]

Widespread hatred of Jonathan Wild and his system probably forced official action against him. With a boldness resulting perhaps from desperation,[30] he had for some time been completely open about his activities, even taking part in robberies himself.[31] Early in 1725 Wild's confederate, Roger Johnson, was arrested; Wild recklessly led a party to the prison, provoked a riot, and helped Johnson escape.[32] For this Wild was arrested and committed to Newgate on February 15, 1725. Somewhat hampered, he continued to direct the stealing and returning of movable property. Very soon after his arrest he accepted ten guineas reward from one Catherine Stetham for restoring some lace stolen by his thieves from her shop. She and two of Wild's old retainers lodged an information against him, and, although still in prison, he was immediately rearrested for a violation of the law of 1718, which made it a felony without benefit of clergy for any person to accept reward for restoring stolen property, unless he apprehended the criminal.[33] The authorities, having finally secured the man who had so successfully evaded them, gave him no chance to escape. He was denied bail and held, well guarded, pending indictment and trial.[34]

After some delay a bill of indictment for felony was found against Jonathan Wild.[35] At his trial there was plentiful evidence against him[36] and very little in his favor. Apparently Wild could not realize that justice was about to overtake him.[37] He admitted his guilt in connection with the theft of lace from Catherine Stetham, but offered in extenuation his services to the state in apprehending criminals. His counsel had circulated in the Old Bailey a printed list of the names of seventy-six criminals discovered, apprehended, and convicted by Jonathan Wild.[38] This did him more harm than good. His request for transportation to the colonies instead of the death penalty was denied, and on May 15 he was sentenced to be hanged at the next regular time of execution, ten days later.[39]

Jonathan Wild's conduct during the period of life remaining to him was disordered and cowardly.[40] On the day before his death he was attended by the Rev. Thomas Purney, Ordinary of Newgate, and the Rev. Mr. Nicholson of St. Sepulchre's Church. After receiving the sacrament Wild asked some confused questions "concerning the Disposition of the soul . . . and the local Situation of the other World, &c."[41] In the evening he asked whether or not suicide were a crime, and, if so, how "the noble *Greeks* & famous *Romans*" became glorious in history. About two o'clock in the morning he tried to commit suicide by drinking laudanum. He made the mistake, however, of taking an overdose and lived.[42]

Almost all London gathered, on the morning of May 24, to watch Wild's progress from Newgate to Tyburn. The poet John Byrom, who watched the procession from Abingdon's Coffee House, gives a vivid description of the scene in "A Letter to R. L. Esq. . . . ":

> Poor *Jonathan Wild!*—Clowes, Peer Williams, and I
> Have just been in waiting to see him pass by:
> Good law! how the Houses were crowded with Mobs,
> That look't like LEVIATHAN's Picture in HOBB's;
> From the very ground Floor to the Top of the Leads,
> While Jonathan past thro' a *Holborn* of Heads.
>
> From *Newgate* to *Tyburn* he made his Procession,
> Supported by two of the nimble Profession;
> Between the unheeded poor Wretches he sat;
> In his Night-gown and Wig, but without e'er a Hat;
> With a Book in his Hand he went weeping and praying,
> The Mob all along, as they passed 'em, huzzaing;
> While a Parcel of Verses the Hawkers were hollowing
> Of which I can only remember these following.
>
> "The cunning old Pug, ev'ry Body remembers,
> "That when he saw Chesnuts roasting i' the Embers,
> "To save his own Bacon, took Puss's two Foots,
> "And so out o' th' Embers he tickled his Nuts,
> "Thus many a poor Rogue has been burnt in the Hand,
> "And 'twas all *Nuts* to *Jonathan,* you understand;
> "But he was not so cunning as Aesop's old Ape,
> "For the Monkey has brought himself into the Scrape."[43]

The account of Jonathan Wild's last appearance written by Defoe, who was undoubtedly present, substantiates Byrom's description:

On Monday, about the usual Time, *Jonathan Wild* was executed at Tyburn. Never was there seen so prodigious a Concourse of People before, not even upon the most popular Occasion of that Nature. The famous *Jack Sheppard* had a tolerable Number to attend his Exit; but no more to be compared to the present, than a Regiment to an Army. And, which is very remarkable, in all that innumerable Crowd, there was not one Pitying Eye to be seen, nor one Compassionate Word to be heard; but, on the contrary, wherever he came, there was nothing but Hollowing and Huzzas, as if it had been upon a Triumph.⁴⁴

Thus died Jonathan Wild, perhaps the first great criminal organizer. He had been hated and feared during his lifetime; it was natural that the populace should greet his death with general rejoicing.

THE "GREAT THIEF'S" REPUTATION

The literature which recorded the career of Jonathan Wild and perpetuated his reputation is of two kinds: the ephemeral—references and catchpenny pamphlets—and the more serious biographies and characterizations, which took various forms. In general, writings of the first type appeared during Wild's lifetime or within a few days after his execution. The serious comments and interpretations, on which Fielding relied more heavily, may be said to date from June, 1725, when Defoe's *Life and Actions of Jonathan Wild* was published. Subsequent uses of Wild's name and reputation were chiefly political in purpose, and so effective was the work of the Opposition writers that by 1743 Wild had become a symbol of evil and cruelty. As such, he appears in Fielding's *Life of Mr. Jonathan Wild the Great.*

Wild's name first came into some prominence in 1718 as the result of an assault made on his character by a former city marshal, Charles Hitchin. While in office Hitchin had filled his pockets with bribes from thieves, shoplifters, highwaymen, prostitutes, and bawdyhouse keepers, and with rewards for supplying information concerning those members of the underworld who refused to buy his protection. At some time during his rise Wild was associated with Hitchin, perhaps as an understudy, perhaps as a partner. After their separation Hitchin apparently lost both his unofficial income and his official position. He revenged himself by attacking Wild in an illiterate pamphlet entitled *The Regulator; or, A Discovery of the Thieves, Thief-Takers, and Locks, alias Receivers of Stolen Goods in and about the City of London. . . .* This squib deals chiefly in abuse. Wild is "King among the Thieves, and Lying-Master General of *England,* Captain General of the Army of Plunderers, and Embassador Extraordinary from the Prince of the Air."[45] Hitchin does make a pretense of being concerned for the public good. He charges that Wild trains young criminals, and gives a list of seventeen *"Thieves that are now at Liberty that are* Jonathan Wild's *Weekly Pensioners."*[46] In an extravagant Proclamation "by his Skittish and Baboonish Majesty" Hitchin reveals Wild's methods of protecting the obedient members of his gang from the law and of hanging the insubordinate ones.[47] He deplores the fact that "the *Thief,* the Gaol, the Justice, and the King's Evidence all . . . seem to be influenced and managed by him . . . "[48] and, amusingly enough, concludes his blast by recommending that Jonathan Wild's iniquities be ended by giving increased power to the city marshal.[49] Certainly more significant, however, is a crude woodcut cartoon of J——W—— hanging from a gibbet, with the words "I'm the Grand Thief" issuing from his mouth.[50] And, indeed, Wild very soon acquired the reputation of being a far greater thief than any of the members of his gang.

A hack writer hired by Wild immediately replied to Hitchin's attack in a pamphlet entitled *An Answer to a Late Insolent Libel entitled a Discovery of the Conduct of Receivers and Thief-Takers. . . .*[51] The defense makes no attempt to deny the specific accusations brought by Hitchin. It discredits the former city marshal, the "Grand Master of Iniquity," by relating incidents in which he proved himself a despicable and ludicrous person. To Hitchin's denunciation of Wild as a public menace the pamphleteer replies at some length with evidences of his employer's great services to the state. The purport of this part of the defense is shown by the following quotation: "'tis highly conspicuous to the sensible part of mankind that evidence and information are the foundation for executing of laws and putting of justice into practice, and without them 'tis impossible that robberies, thefts, or other villanies can be suppressed."[52]

This exchange of incivilities, although not important in itself, marks the beginning of Jonathan Wild's notoriety.[53] A letter printed in *Mist's Weekly Journal* late in 1719 continues the attack by referring to several witty proposals to give the recently vacated place of ordinary of Newgate to the "scandalous *Jonathan W[il]d*."[54] Captain Alexander Smith probably referred to Jonathan Wild also when he wrote in *The Thieves Grammar:* "The most special Rules to be observed by Thieves in their Art of Grammar, is for them not be too familiar with a Thief-Taker. . . ."[55] Earlier in this pamphlet Smith observed: "Note, that a *Thief,* a *Thief-taker,* a *Bailiff,* a *Serjeant,* and his Yeoman, are Correlatives, or at least Synonimous, that is to say, every one of those Names signifies a great Rogue, but of them all, *Grammarians* not inferiour to *Gellius, Quintilian,* or *Macrobius* holds the Thief to be the Honestest Man."[56]

As Jonathan Wild became more notorious such references multiplied. The most interesting of these are the various tales of his encounters with Blueskin and Jack Sheppard, whose deaths Jonathan Wild engineered. The biographers of Blake and of Wild, for example, almost unanimously praise Blueskin for his attempt on Wild's life and regret that Wild survived. Defoe pretends to quote Jack Sheppard as saying that "nothing but the cutting of Jonathan Wild's throat could have made him [Blueskin] so considerable."[57] Swift made this incident the subject of his very popular "Blueskin's Ballad." The first two stanzas read:

> Ye Fellows of Newgate whose Fingers are nice
> In diving of Pockets and Cogging of Dice;
> Ye Sharpers so rich who can buy off the Noose,

Ye honester poor Rogues who die in your Shoes,
Attend and draw near.
Good news you shall hear.—
How Honest *Wild's* Throat was cut from Ear to Ear.
Now *Blueskin's* sharp Penknife has set you at Ease,
And ev'ry Man round me may rob if he please.

When to the Old Bailey this *Blueskin* was led,
He held up his Hands, his Indictment was Read,
Loud rattled his Chains, near him honest *Wild* stood,
For full Forty Pounds was the Price of his Blood.
Then hopeless of Life
He drew his Penknife
And made a sad Widow of honest *Wild's* Wife.
But forty Pounds paid her, her Grief shall appease
And ev'ry Man round me may rob if he please.[58]

The ballads and letters concerning Wild and Sheppard clearly show the effect of Sheppard's execution[59] upon Jonathan Wild's reputation. Defoe wrote two lives of Sheppard. One, *The History of the Remarkable Life of John Sheppard,* is a straightforward biography. The second, *A Narrative of all the Robberies, Escapes, &c. of John Sheppard,* a canting, sensationalized account, purports to be Sheppard's "confession."[60] Toward the end of it Sheppard makes a statement obviously directed at Wild:

I have often lamented the scandalous practice of thief-taking, as it is called, and the public manner of offering rewards for stolen goods, in defiance of two several Acts of Parliament, the thief-catchers living sumptuously, and keeping of public offices of intelligence: these, who forfeit their lives every day they breathe, and deserve the gallows as richly as any of the thieves, send us as their representatives to Tyburn once a month; thus they hang by proxy while we do it fairly in person.[61]

Soon after Sheppard's death John Thurmond simultaneously staged, at the Drury Lane Theatre, and published a pantomime entitled *Harlequin Sheppard; A Night Scene in Grotesque Characters.*[62] The dumb show presents first one of Sheppard's unsuccessful attempts to escape from Newgate. Following that is a reënactment of Blueskin's assault on Wild. Blueskin and all the prisoners of

Newgate are overjoyed by what they believe to have been a successful throat-cutting.[63]

The decline of Wild's reputation can be seen even more clearly in the anonymous play entitled *The Prison-Breaker; or, the Adventures of John Sheppard,* written for presentation at the Theatre-Royal in Lincoln's Inn Fields, and printed early in 1725.[64] Jonathan Wile [sic], a Thief-Taker, has a prominent part in the action, being, as in life, the chief cause of Sheppard's death. In his first appearance on the stage Jonathan Wile is shown as being heartless, cunning, and cynically humorous:

> JON. Well, when you see him [Sheppard], remember my Love to him. I can't stay with you now, for I must go and drink with the Fellows I condemn'd last Sessions, they dye to-Morrow. And you Know, old Friends must part as Friends.
>
> RUST. You are very Kind to 'em, Mr. *Wile.*
>
> JON. Ay, so you'd say, if you Knew all. I'll engage it costs me a Crown at least, every Execution Day in treating one or another of 'em. Besides the Loss of my Time, attending 'em at the Tree; For I love to see the last of 'em...[65]

In the remainder of the play Sheppard escapes from prison, rejoins his gang, but is treacherously recaptured by Wile. In the final scene, as the two reënter Newgate, Sheppard bids Wile this adieu: "But when it [hanging] happens, I am sure I shan't leave so great a Villain upon Earth as myself, unless it be your Worship. So fare you well, and be damned."[66]

His "Worship" was not long in following Sheppard to Newgate and Tyburn. By the time of Wild's imprisonment popular interest was so great that the first of two leading articles condemning him appeared in *The British Journal* a week after his first arrest. The author of these unsigned articles was Bernard Mandeville.[67] The first, "Of Theftbote;[68] or, the Crime of Compounding Felony," deals with the harm done to society by "our shameful Negotiations with Thieves, or their Agents, for the Recovery of stolen Goods, by which, in Reality, we become Aiders and Abetters to them."[69]

Jonathan Wild is cited as the great offender in compounding felony, and his methods are scornfully revealed. Mandeville concludes:

It is highly criminal in any Man, for Lucre, to connive at a Piece of Felony which he could have hinder'd. But a profess'd Thief-Catcher, above all, ought to be severely punished, if it can be proved that he has suffered a known Rogue to go on in his Villainy, tho' but one Day, after it was in his Power to apprehend and convict him, more especially if it appears that he was a Sharer in the Profit.[70]

The second article, "Of the ill Consequences of Theftbote," discusses the second charge in the popular bill of particulars against Wild—his ruthless management of the gang. Again Mandeville exposes Wild's methods of controlling his men, and summarizes thus:

A licens'd Practitioner may be skreen'd and protected some Years, if he sticks to Discipline, and pays the greatest Part of his Earnings for his Security; but if he rides resty, and squabbles about the Contributions required of him, he is in a dangerous Way. It is possible that a dextrous Youth may be esteemed, and be a Favourite to the Superintendent a great while, but when he grows very notorious he is hunted like a Deer, and the Premium on his Head betrays him. . . . A Thief bred must be hang'd if he lives.[71]

This paper, an eloquent indictment, doubtless recalled Blueskin and Sheppard to the popular mind.

The hanging of Jonathan Wild was followed immediately by the hasty publication of all manner of "last speeches," "last farewells," "epitaphs," "elegies," broadside ballads, and catchpenny biographies, each one purportedly full of new and sensational facts. Defoe states that accounts of Wild "would make up a large volume folio, and yet leave many unrelated."[72] Most of this ephemeral literature was forgotten within a month, and much of it is now lost. From what has remained it is possible to identify its chief characteristics.

Several pieces of miscellaneous verse are interesting for their tone of jeering exultation. The writer for *Mist's Weekly Journal* who watched the execution composed a doggerel account of Jonathan's arrival in the lower world. As soon as Jonathan leaps from the boat he is attacked by Blueskin, and barely escapes. The poem continues with Jonathan's explanation of his wounds, and ends with a palpable hit:

> For this Wound in my Forehead I'll make Affidavit,
> (If *Minos* is fitting), that I myself gave it.
> Then how came your Neck broke, the Devils cry'd all.
> Saith he, For my Neck, that was broke by a Fall.[73]

An anonymous "elegy" opens with a salute to the hanging tree at Tyburn:

> Hail rev'rend Tripos, Triple Tree of State,
> Who arbitrates the grand decrees of Fate,
> And is the chief defender of the laws,
> Three Kingdoms joyfully give thee applause,
> And universal praises to thee sing,
> Since Jonathan upon thy beams did swing.[74]

Another versifier proposes to dip his pen in Lethe before writing about Jonathan Wild—

> For none (I think) can write of him so well
> But what is brought from the confines of Hell.[75]

Slightly more polished is the single sheet poem "England's Ingratitude; or, Jonathan Wild's Complaint." The scene is Wild's "dreary cell" in Newgate, a few days before his execution. Jonathan, soliloquizing, complains bitterly against the country which has forgotten his services and the hazards he encountered in hanging "thrice thirty" of the nation's enemies. He predicts that the day will come when England will wish him alive again, and concludes with a long exhortation to his disciples, the satire of which is obvious:

> But you, my faithful servants everywhere,
> Whom I have train'd up with a father's care,
> Sure you some grateful sentiments will have,
> And drop a tear upon your master's grave.
>
> • • •
>
> You by me were made
> Successful artists in the thieving trade;
> I taught ye to lead comfortable lives,

> To keep a train of whores, and starve your wives;
> Go on and prosper, bravely play your parts,
> Nor leave unpractis'd any of your arts!
> Be rogues renown'd, and trample on the laws,
> And like true bloods, revenge your patron's cause.[76]

A third poetic treatment of Jonathan Wild is in an anonymous biographical sketch entitled *Weighley, alias Wild,* written in Hudibrastic couplets.[77] This informal life recounts the beginning of Wild's criminal career in Wolverhampton, traces his flight to London, tells of his imprisonment for robbery, and of his marriage to a Tyburn widow. Wild's organization of a gang is dramatized in an elaborate mock-heroic banquet scene, in which Wild and the thieves swear eternal fellowship. A few lines later the thieves are shown as dissatisfied and disposed to conspire with Madame Wild to impeach their leader. Accordingly, Jonathan is captured, convicted, and hanged. This highly fictionalized account is interesting chiefly because of the rough satire which pervades the whole. For example:

> Accouter'd well our Hero trudg'd on,
> With Pistols charg'd, with Sword & Gun;
> And to be sure he oft did quiver,
> When he cry'd first, *stand, deliver!*
> But as he went oft, oft did speed
> And so grew harden'd in his Trade.[78]

The satirical versified biography is followed by an epitaph, a defiant farewell, and a "ballad," all of which moralize on Jonathan's career in a perfectly straightforward, gloomy fashion.

Appended to the poetic section is a sensationalized, non-satirical prose life which embellishes the usual biographical pattern with such fanciful details as that Wild was born deformed and hideous and that he once sliced off Mary Milliner's ear to silence her chiding. Such lurid creations of a scribbler's invention are common in early eighteenth-century criminal biography.

Another piece in which satire prevails is the anonymous *News from the Dead; or, A Dialogue between Blueskin, Shepperd, and Jonathan Wild.* In this feeble imitation of a Lucianic dialogue

Blueskin and Jack Sheppard again welcome Jonathan Wild to the underworld,[79] and ask him for news of the world above. Jonathan rehearses his trial, attempted suicide, and progress to Tyburn, but tries to deny having been hanged.[80] He then becomes eager to know what employment he will be given in the lower regions, and asks Sheppard's "interest" in becoming either a justice of the peace or thief-taker general. His hope is futile; he has been designated as a tub-preacher whose duty will be to "hold forth every Day among those disaffected Souls the Fanaticks."[81] Further conversation is interrupted by the sounding of a great bell, which, Blueskin tells Jonathan, is the signal for all new arrivals to appear before Minos to receive sentence. The irony in this squib consists in emphasizing the similarity between the underworld and the world above and in making Jonathan Wild acknowledge with complete candor his own mendacity, villainy, and cowardice.

Of the numerous lives of Wild written and published soon after his death, the most detailed and most relevant is Daniel Defoe's *True and Genuine Account of the Life and Actions of the late Jonathan Wild; not Made up out of Fiction & Fable, but Taken from his own Mouth, and Collected from Papers of his own Writing.*[82] Fielding undoubtedly refers to Defoe and to this work when he mentions "that excellent Historian, who from authentic Papers and Records, &c. hath already given so satisfactory an Account of the Life and Actions of this Great Man."[83] Unlike most of the scribblers, Defoe did not put his biography of Wild before the public on execution day. He withheld publication and advertised widely that he had in progress not a catchpenny life, but a complete, authentic, and serious study of the famous criminal. On June 8 the publisher John Applebee released the first edition; a second edition appeared on June 10, and a third on June 12.[84] In the preface Defoe, in a fashion which we have come to recognize as typical of him, abuses the earlier "absurd and ridiculous accounts," on which, as a matter of fact, he probably relied heavily, and sets himself up in contrast to the scribblers as a serious moral historian:

The following tract does not indeed make a jest of his story as they do, or present his history, which indeed is a tragedy of itself, in a style of mockery and ridicule, but in a method agreeable to the fact. They that had rather have a falsehood to laugh at than a true account of things to inform them, had best buy the fiction, and leave the history to those who know how to distinguish good from evil.[85]

The amount of actual information about the life of Jonathan Wild to be found in Defoe's biography is not great. In fact, Defoe used biographical data merely as a starting point for his extended remarks on two subjects of greater interest—Jonathan Wild's character and his methods of directing a criminal syndicate.

Defoe's opinion of Wild's character was officially, of course, utterly damning: "[his] was a life of horrid and inimitable wickedness." But Defoe found in Jonathan Wild more than simple wickedness. He had to grant that the villain had "a kind of brutal courage," which might better be labeled boldness or impudence. Certainly, in view of "his stupid and confused behaviour during his lying in Newgate and at his execution," he could not be called a brave man. But for Wild's purposes boldness and impudence were probably more useful than bravery.[86] His audacity was further demonstrated by his skill in imposing upon people. Although utterly selfish, Wild constantly maintained his hypocritical pose as a public servant and as a friend to victims of theft, even when popular opinion had repudiated him. Defoe gives several instances of Wild's ability to convince doubters of his honesty. This he did by being straightforward, bluff, and, when necessary, rude in his speech and manner. Unfortunately for Wild, however, his plausibility and audacity were not accompanied by prudence. He became intent on nothing but plunder and gain. As Defoe puts it, "in a word, Jonathan's avarice hanged him."[87] Defoe's portraits of Jack Sheppard, Captain Gow, Captain Avery, Duncan Campbell, Captain Singleton, and Quaker William all show traces either of sympathy or of a not unfriendly tolerance, for Defoe pretended to condone mere roguery. But Jonathan Wild did not fit this formula; to Defoe he was not a rogue but a villain.

To a large extent Defoe's exposition of Wild's methods supplements his characterization. He points out that Wild's profession—encouraging thievery, receiving and returning stolen goods, and impeaching all non-conforming felons—did not require him to expose himself to danger. Defoe makes a considerable study of Wild's ability to deceive. One of the most entertaining passages in the biography is a series of imaginary conversations between Wild and a lady whose jeweled watch has been stolen by one of Wild's operators. At the end of these negotiations the lady forces a present of fifteen guineas on the "reluctant" thief-taker. The one feature of Wild's system which Defoe found more hateful than any other was his way of training up youths to be members of his gang. Defoe examines this practice at some length, and concludes with a passage of unusual vehemence: "First to tempt and then accuse, which is the very nature of the devil; first to make poor desolate vagabond boys thieves, and then betray them to the gallows! Who can think of such a thing without a just abhorrence? Who can think it to be less than the worst sort of murder?"[88] Defoe concludes his analysis of Wild's system by describing its gradual breakdown, which accompanied the growing greed that was his ruin.

Moral seriousness pervades Defoe's biography. Almost every page contains a warning, expressed or implied, against the wicked course of life which Wild exemplified. This mood is augmented by the circumstantial and sensational realism which makes Defoe's works, whether true history or pure fiction, convincing. There is no way of ascertaining just how faithful to fact Defoe's biography of Jonathan Wild is, and its reliability is here a minor question. The important thing is that Defoe left the first coherent interpretation of Jonathan Wild as a man. Hypocrisy and cruel selfishness are the elements of Wild's character which Defoe emphasizes. This conception of the man soon gained such wide currency that Jonathan Wild became virtually a symbol of human baseness. Defoe chose to express his hatred of all that Jonathan Wild represented in terms of vigorous and straightforward damnation. Other writers treated Wild in a spirit of elaborate irony, in which hatred of the symbol is always apparent.[89] For the most part, between 1725 and 1743 the satirical attitude toward Wild prevailed. Both attitudes are to be found in Fielding's *Life of Mr. Jonathan Wild the Great*.

As W. L. Cross points out, "had the story of Jonathan Wild remained where Defoe left it, it would have been . . . forgotten."[90] But at the time of Wild's death the Opposition, headed by Bolingbroke, Carteret, Pulteney, and Wyndham, was organizing its literary campaign against Walpole, and was therefore in search of satirical symbols to represent the Prime Minister. The correspondence between Wild's reputation and the conception of Walpole's character which the Opposition wished to establish was too close to be neglected.[91] "He [Walpole] was represented," writes M. D. Hessler, "as a vain and ambitious statesman who aimed at arbitrary power and was absolutely ruthless and shameless in his methods of achieving it."[92] Recent historians, unswayed by partisanship, have demonstrated that, despite his methods, Walpole was really a good minister of state. The Opposition writers, however, were interested not in calm truth, but in defamation; to this end their campaign was ruthless and frequently unfair.

A number of literary devices were employed by writers for the Opposition in the course of their unremitting attack on the Prime Minister. One of the most common of these consisted in drawing a parallel between a corrupt and avaricious statesman and a bold thief, often with ironical praise of such "great men." The resemblance between Jonathan Wild, the hated thief and thief-taker, and the Prime Minister, although too dangerous to state in unequivocal terms, was not lost on a public expert in reading political satire.[93] The frequent use of Wild's name by Opposition satirists soon obscured in the popular memory the details of his career and character. There remained instead a simplified conception of Wild as a selfish, hypocritical robber, intent on victimizing the public.

Jonathan Swift recognized the spiritual kinship between Wild and Walpole during Wild's lifetime, and some months before the Opposition writers became aware of the satirical value of the comparison.[94] In "Blueskin's Ballad," mentioned previously, the Dean makes much of the fact that Blueskin's attack on "honest Wild" ensures the safety not only of the little rogues who pick pockets and rob on the highway, but also of the great rogues who "rob in the Customs . . . [and] cheat in the 'cise." One stanza undoubtedly points directly to Walpole:

> Some say there are Courtiers of highest Renown
> Who steal the King's Gold and leave him but a Crown;
> Some say there are Peers and some Parliament Men
> Who meet once a Year to rob Courtiers again;
> But let them have their swing
> To pillage the King,
> And get a blue Ribbon instead of a string
> For *Blueskin's* sharp, &c.[95]

There are no noteworthy political connotations in the poems and pamphlets evoked by Wild's execution. Very soon after the excitement in Grub Street subsided, however, there appeared an unmistakable piece of Opposition propaganda. This was a long, mock-serious essay on the private life and opinions of Jonathan Wild, "that celebrated Statesman and Politician," supposedly written by an acquaintance. It was printed in two parts on May 12 and May 19, 1725,[96] as the leading article in *Mist's Weekly Journal,* an Opposition newspaper established two months earlier.[97] Jonathan Wild, whom the writer affects to venerate as a "great man,"[98] is said to have believed that "Men of Parts . . . should be maintained by the Publick . . . whether it was done by picking their Pockets, or boldly by taking their money by Force. . . ."[99] He thought his own age most fortunate, since "a Man's Thriving and growing great in the World" is no longer hindered by such foolish prejudices as "Honour and Conscience, which now . . . your busy pushing People look upon to be Chimeras. . . ."[100] According to this account, it was Jonathan's settled conviction that men of parts and wit are by nature privileged to use mankind as they wish, but that fools and projectors, who can do no more than cheat their equals in South-Sea schemes, should never be admitted to the exalted company of rogues. Jonathan also planned to commission the author of the *Fable of the Bees* to write a "treatise . . . *de Legibus Naturae;* under which Title, Theft, and all kinds of Knavery should be recommended as virtuous and honourable Actions...."[101] This treatise would supposedly supplement a "History of his own Times," written by Jonathan Wild himself and containing many state secrets, which was to be published seven years after his death. The concluding paragraph of this essay on Jonathan Wild cŏntains the writer's most vigorous stroke of political satire. It reads: "As to Religion, he was a Freethinker, and I'm afraid, a little inclin'd to *Atheism*.... As to Party, he was both in Principle and Practice a right modern Whig, according to the Definition of those Gentlemen, which is express'd in their Motto— *Keep what you get, and get what you can*."[102]

This sketch contains most of the tricks employed by the Opposition writers in drawing the thief-statesman parallel. Walpole's arbitrariness and corruption—the two fundamental charges in the Opposition's bill of particulars[103]—are clearly revealed to a knowing reader. The satire is double in effect: the rogue is ridiculed by pretended elevation, the politician by degradation. And the incongruity of the parallel is heightened by the serious, straightforward language in which the piece is written.

This essay is unquestionably the work of an accomplished satirist, but as yet its author is unidentified. When Alfred E. Robbins discovered the "Mist articles," he promptly credited them to Fielding, seeing in them the germ of *Jonathan Wild*.[104] J. Paul de Castro conceded the great resemblance between the two, which is occasionally apparent even in phraseology, but contended that Henry Fielding —in 1725 just eighteen years old and recently out of Eton—could not and would not have written such a sketch.[105] Either Swift or Defoe, he suggested, is a much more likely candidate for authorship. De Castro's case is undoubtedly stronger than Robbins',[106] although he neglects to mention another possibility, John Gay. Whatever the identity of the anonymous satirist, Fielding apparently knew his work. It is highly probable that these are the "short Memoirs, which about the Time of his Death were published in certain Chronicles called Newspapers . . ."[107] which Fielding, in the Preface to the *Miscellanies*, admits having seen.

A more elaborate use of the satirical technique of the "Mist articles" is to be found throughout *The Beggar's Opera,* which began its famous run in January, 1728. It has long been recognized that the career of Jonathan Wild was one of the unwritten sources which Gay found most valuable both for the Newgate setting and for the political satire of his play. It has even been strongly suggested that Gay may have enjoyed some personal acquaintance with the thief-taker.[108]

Jonathan Wild's presence in *The Beggar's Opera* was immediately recognized. "Phil-Harmonicus," writing in *The Craftsman,* notes: "In the very first Song, the Employment of a *Statesman* is, by *innuendo,* made as bad or worse than that of *Jonathan Wild,* represented under the Character of Peachum. . . ."[109]

This "very first Song," which opens the action, provides a good starting point for an analysis of the relationship of Peachum and his original. It reads:

> Through all the Employments of Life
>   Each Neighbour abuses his Brother;
> Whore and Rogue they call Husband and Wife;
>   All Professions be-rogue one another:
> The Priest calls the Lawyer a Cheat,
>   The Lawyer be-Knaves the Divine:
> And the Statesman, because he's so great,
>   Thinks his Trade as honest as mine.[110]

Peachum continues with a speech which would, for an audience of 1728, identify his prototype and forecast his character: "A Lawyer is an honest Employment, so is mine. Like me too he acts in a double Capacity, both against Rogues and for 'em; for 'tis but fitting that we should protect and encourage Cheats, since we live by them."[111]

Peachum's dramatic nature is not very elaborately developed throughout the rest of the action. He remains a heartless, completely self-interested, cynically humorous, "great" rogue, somewhat reminiscent of Jonathan Wile in *The Prison-Breaker.*[112] Many of the details which fill out this portrait of Peachum are drawn from

Jonathan Wild's known methods. The thief-taker promises to "soften the evidence" against Black Moll because "the wench is active and industrious."[113] But he gladly hears that Tom Gagg is found guilty and records in advance the forty pounds reward which his death will bring.[114] One victim, it appears, is not sufficient. Peachum goes over his whole roster of thieves, commenting on each, in search of "a decent Execution against next Sessions," and selects for impeachment all his unprofitable, rebellious pensioners.[115] In the revelation of Peachum's business practices there are also several details which resemble actual practices of Jonathan Wild. Peachum instructs his wife[116] to "rip out the Coronets and Marks of these Dozen of Cambric Handkerchiefs," so that they may be sold.[117] When Peachum hears a customer entering, that is, an inquirer after stolen property, he cautions Polly to put him off with excuses.[118] Peachum obviously has "hands" at work at all public gatherings. Particularly rewarding are court assemblies:

> LOCKIT. The Coronation Account, Brother Peachum, is of so intricate a nature, that I believe it will never be settled.
>
> PEACHUM. It consists indeed of a great Variety of Articles.—It was worth to our People, in Fees of different kinds, above ten Instalments. . . .[119]

In addition to using biographical minutiae, Gay was careful to attribute to Peachum those actions and attitudes which his audience would expect from one of Jonathan Wild's reputation. Peachum seeks to hang Macheath, Polly's husband, because such a son-in-law is dangerous, and because, as he sees it, a widow's jointure is the only profit which Polly can expect from so imprudent a marriage. At the same time, "it grieves [his] Heart to take off [such] a great Man," from whose robberies he has profited to a considerable extent.[120] Having made his resolution, Peachum does not scruple to use treachery in capturing Macheath.[121] When he seems certainly due for the gallows, Peachum has only cynical consolation for his distracted daughter: "Set your Heart at rest, Polly.—Your Husband is to die today.—Therefore if you are not already provided, 'tis high time to look about for another. There's Comfort for you, you Slut."[122] In short, Peachum is as cruel, selfish, cunning, and greedy a villain as Jonathan Wild was ever made out to be.

It may be objected that a serious interpretation of Peachum's character disregards Gay's obvious comic intention. From the point of view of the dramatic conflict alone, however, Peachum represents the forces of evil. Despite the fact that political and social satire pervades *The Beggar's Opera* and sets its tone, sentimentality and melodrama are present in sufficient strength to modify the whole. *The Beggar's Opera* is no bitter Juvenalian indictment of man and society; it is rather an eighteenth century version of the "toothless satire." The melodramatic and sentimental motif is provided by a pair of appealing, if not precisely winsome, lovers, who are opposed, thwarted, and virtually persecuted by one who is intent on destroying their happiness. No amount of low comedy and satire could detract from the audience's sentimental interest in such a situation, a fact which is made plain by the reception which Polly and Macheath received.[123] The surprising reprieve with which Gay averted "downright deep Tragedy" is an effective device for making fun of the inevitable "happy ending" of opera. But it is also a means of sparing the sensibilities of the audience. For, although he is treated humorously, Peachum, like Jonathan Wild, is an undeniable villain. And even the authors who ridiculed Wild were motivated by hatred of the evil which he symbolized.

In the satire on Walpole in *The Beggar's Opera*,[124] as in the "Mist articles," the villain and the politician, both "great men," are equated, to the disadvantage of the latter. Swift, in a paper defending Gay against charges of undermining public morality, clearly states the essential point:

This comedy contains likewise a satire which, although it doth by no means affect the present age, yet might have been useful in the former, and may possibly be so in ages to come. I mean where the author takes occasion of comparing those common robbers to robbers of the public; and their several stratagems of betraying, undermining, and hanging each other to the several arts of politicians in times of corruption.[125]

The device of drawing an elaborate comparison between "common robbers" and "robbers of the public," so effectively employed in *The Beggar's Opera*,[126] was adopted by the two foremost journals of the Opposition, *The Craftsman* and *Common Sense*. *The Craftsman*, begun in 1726 under the patronage of Lord Bolingbroke and managed and written largely by Nicholas Amhurst,[127] made the thief-statesman parallel, in one form or another, familiar to all its readers. A letter from "Jack Hinter" ironically condemns *The Beggar's Opera* for "setting forth publick Robbers as Heroes."[128] According to another paper, "the *wicked Politician* only stands erect by himself in the first and highest Rank of Plunderers; and seems, in his Prosperity, to look down and despise the Law, which he has broken."[129] Still another asks "what Reasons can We have to suppose that a Man, who plunders a whole Nation without Remorse, would not, in a lower Sphere, pick a Pocket, or take a Purse on the Road . . . ?"[130] The appendix to the 1729 volume contains "Polly Peachum: a New Ballad," one stanza of which reads:

> Great Dames there are, who break their Vows
>   As oft as Madam *Peachum,*
> And *greater Robbers* than her Spouse
>   Tho' Tyburn cannot reach 'em.[131]

The name of Jonathan Wild is not used in this anti-Walpole crusade as often as one might expect. It is probable, however, that the memory of Jonathan Wild's reputation recurred to the reader with each paper which insisted on the resemblance between a thief and a corrupt politician or courtier. Occasionally the parallel is made explicit. "Anti-Screen," an Opposition author,[132] writing after Walpole's resignation from office in February, 1742, observes that "*To be true to the Gang,* is a Maxim which has obtain'd in other Offices besides *Jonathan Wild's*. . . ." He goes on to suggest, probably with reference to the Parliamentary investigation of Walpole's activities,[133] that anyone who "should boggle in his evidence . . . only proves that he himself is *one of his Gang*."[134] In a later number, Wild's name occurs again, this time in company with Colonel Charteris and Oliver Cromwell, as an example of a great hypocrite.[135]

The satirical thief-statesman comparison and direct reference to Jonathan Wild are employed even more frequently in *Common Sense; or, The Englishman's Journal*, the weekly sheet founded in February, 1737, by Lord Chesterfield and Lord Lyttelton, two of the leaders of that group of the Opposition called the Patriots.[136] The Preface announces that the raillery to be discovered in the articles which follow "diverts itself with the Follies of great Criminals, such Criminals as Laws cannot, or at least do not punish. . . ."[137] The essay for July 30, 1737, reviews the career of the highwayman Dick Turpin, and attributes his continued success to the paralysis of England's public spirit. The political application of this is obvious.[138] A postscript in the issue of November 17, 1738, prints a speech delivered by "Bob Booty" [Walpole] to his rebellious gang. Bob points out that while the rogue at the bar is despised, the same rogue on the bench would be feared. His peroration, expressed in Newgate slang, warns them: "If you fancy that, by giving me up, you may slip your own necks out of the halter, you are bit.—If it is decreed, that I must swing . . . I'll peach every knave and fool among you, that is to say, the whole gang here present, d——m my eyes if I don't and so look to it."[139] It is not difficult to imagine Jonathan Wild haranguing his villainous crew in much the same manner.

About a month later the weekly essayist announces that he will "lay aside Politicks" for one issue, and entertain his readers instead "with some Memoirs of the Life of a certain great Man, deceas'd."[140] The writer's pretense of laying politics aside is amusingly transparent, since his subject is Jonathan Wild, whose resemblance to Sir Robert Walpole is, as usual, obliquely indicated. According to this vignette, Wild at one time "seem'd rather born to a Ribband around his Shoulders, than to a Rope about his Neck." He held levees, at which he received persons of quality with an "awkward Familiarity," and fleeced them all. Professional success and the condescension of his fine company made him "insufferably arrogant," and he maintained a lordly establishment until he was hanged. The writer supplements these observations with a sketch of Wild's life, in which his rise to power and his methods of gaining absolute control of the thieving fraternity are rehearsed. The essay ends with an appraisal of Wild as a man:

> He was certainly a Man of Parts; and had he set out in the World in an honest, instead of a dishonest Road, we might have seen him reckon'd a Patriot, instead of a Pickpocket.... One almost regrets that such a Man should be lost in such a Cause; and yet, as long as this Nation and Language subsists, Infamy and Reproach will be affix'd to the Name of Jonathan Wild.[141]

This reëxamination of Jonathan's career and fame is important, not only because it again brought his name before the notice of a large number of readers, but also because, like Defoe's biography, it is one of the few studies in which there is a genuine attempt to arrive at an understanding of the thief-taker's character.

The tone of the essay in *Common Sense* differs, however, from that of Defoe's life and other pieces of execution literature. The authors writing in 1725 hated and feared Wild the man, and damned him. But the author of this essay has no hatred or fear of a thief hanged thirteen years before. He is merely amused to reveal the true nature of one who for a long period imposed on the public, and moved to regret the misuse of such undeniable talents as Wild possessed. But despite these talents, the writer is careful to say, the "name of *Jonathan Wild*" will always bear a shameful connotation. Here is one of the clearest examples of the popular tendency to regard Jonathan Wild not as a man but as a symbol of human infamy.[142]

Two more specific references to Jonathan Wild occur in *Common Sense*. One appears in a paper on Oliver Cromwell's high-handed methods of dealing with Parliament, a thinly disguised attack on Walpole's arbitrariness. The writer playfully advances the notion that had Jonathan Wild and his gang usurped control of the House of Commons and made laws, even those laws might have been obeyed, but no longer "than till the people should have strength and courage to seize upon *Jonathan* and the whole gang, and hang them all up."[143] The other reference occurs in some exultant reflections on the late administration, published after Walpole's fall. Predicting that Walpole's departure from office will cause the collapse of his whole system, the author refers to "the late Mr. Jonathan Wilde" as another "Instance of what a Misfortune it is to a Family to lose its Head." He goes on to say that Wild left behind a disconsolate widow as well as several other dependent ladies and their issue; and so rapidly was he taken off that he was unable to provide for them, although they certainly deserved some settlement "much better than the Family and Friends of another Person that shall be nameless." The nameless person, of course, is Sir Robert Walpole. The reflections end with a straightforward statement of the comparison which the Patriot writers had found so effective in satire: "all the People upon Earth must have an Abhorrence for those Times, where one Criminal is hang'd for taking a Groat upon the Road, and another honour'd for stealing a Million in an office."[144]

The foregoing discussion of the Opposition satirists' treatment of thieves in general and of Jonathan Wild in particular shows the manner in which biographical material was simplified. Most of the details of Wild's life were forgotten as soon as the writings published at the time of his death passed into oblivion. The specific facts that were remembered were those which the Opposition writers found valuable in their portrayal of Wild as the spiritual brother of a greedy and tyrannical politician. References to Wild were frequent and needed no explanation. A writer in the *Weekly Miscellany* could complain that the stage displayed a "Group of Rogues formed from the Characters of Shepherd, Jonathan Wild [&] Blueskin. . . ."[145] Pope could be certain that his readers understood him when he wrote:

> Down, down, proud Satire! tho' a realm be spoil'd
> Arraign no mightier thief than wretched Wild.[146]

Jonathan Wild's name had become a symbol of the infamous and contemptible. The way had been prepared for Henry Fielding to use "the great thief" as the central figure in an ambitious moral satire.

FIELDING ON JONATHAN WILD

There is, of course, no way of determining the extent or accuracy of Fielding's knowledge of Jonathan Wild. He admits his acquaintance with a biography which was undoubtedly Defoe's;[147] with certain newspaper memoirs, among them probably the "Mist articles";[148] and with the account published by the ordinary of Newgate.[149] Jonathan Wild had achieved notoriety during Fielding's youth. It is reasonable to believe that, in the country as well as in London, Fielding could easily have acquainted himself at first hand with the salient facts of the thief-taker's life and death. *The Enquiry into the Causes of the late Increase of Robbers,* the *Charge delivered to the Grand Jury,* and other works which Fielding wrote during his magistracy reveal a thorough knowledge of London low-life. Fielding's interest in crime and social amelioration undoubtedly antedates his appointment to the Bow Street Court; likewise, he doubtless began his investigation of social conditions well before *Jonathan Wild* was written.

There are in Fielding's *Jonathan Wild* occasional uses of genuine biographical material. Fielding's hero is distrustful of his gang: "he was thoroughly convinced there was not a single Man amongst them, who would not, for the Value of five Shillings bring him to the Gallows."[150] The original Wild put no faith in the unenforced loyalty of his men, and was, indeed, finally hanged on evidence provided by two of them.[151] The immediate cause of Wild's downfall in Fielding's history is "a Clause in an Act of Parliament," by which "it was made Capital in a Prig to steal with the Hands of other People." This law was obviously passed to bring about Wild's destruction, and he could not escape from it.[152] This is roughly what happened to the real Jonathan Wild. Fielding used the story of Blueskin's assault on Wild, altering it to suit his purpose. Blueskin refuses to surrender to Wild a gold watch stolen at Windsor. Wild's appeals to Blueskin's gratitude and loyalty are met with surly refusals. Therefore, that very evening, Wild apprehends the rebellious thief and commits him to Newgate with enough evidence to hang him thrice over. At the time Blueskin is convicted, Wild, "with that disregard and Indifference which GREAT MEN are too carelessly inclined to have for those whom they have ruined," is standing near him and receives from his penknife a wound which is almost fatal. Fortune, however, has decreed that Wild be hanged, and so preserves him for that end.[153]

Fielding made similar use of other biographical facts. Roger Johnson, the smuggler in charge of Wild's international dealings, is introduced as the ruler of Newgate whom Wild finally deposes.[154] The historical Wild and Johnson were doubtless confederates, but it is most unlikely that they were ever in Newgate together.[155] Fielding also expanded the accounts of Wild's interview with the ordinary of Newgate into a farcical dialogue in which the clergyman, befuddled by the punch which Jonathan orders, delivers a violent and senseless harangue on the text *"To the Greeks Foolishness."*[156] Fielding's hero, like his original, wishes to decline "the public Honours she [Fortune] intended him," and attempts to commit suicide by taking laudanum. He found, however, "that to struggle against this Lady's Decrees is vain and impotent: And whether she hath determined you shall be hanged or be a Prime Minister it is in either Case lost Labour to resist."[157] On the appointed morning Jonathan rode from Newgate to Tyburn, amid "the Acclamations of the Multitude, who were highly ravished with his GREATNESS." So anxious were they to witness the apotheosis of Jonathan Wild that they could not wait for the ordinary to perform the last offices, and "began to batter the Cart with Stones, Brickbats, Dirt, and all Manner of Mischievous Weapons." The reverend gentleman retreated, and "with universal Applause our Hero swung out of this World."[158] Fielding thus turned to his satirical purpose the hatred expressed by the mob when Wild was hanged in 1725.[159]

It will be noticed that Fielding used genuine biographical details only toward the conclusion of his history, when the life of his hero was rapidly approaching a melodramatic end. Perhaps Fielding felt that only these latter days of the original Wild's life were sufficiently spectacular to figure in an ironically heroic history of a "great man." Except in those instances mentioned, Fielding paid little attention to biographical facts, although he did find the general outlines of Jonathan's life useful as a framework for his history.

Into this framework Fielding fitted numerous invented characters, incidents, and circumstances necessary to transform the lifestory of Jonathan Wild into a coherent satirical moral narrative. Jonathan is given an illustrious ancestry of prigs, that is, thieves, a line whose founder was picking pockets in Saxon times. He is born in Covent-Garden Roundhouse, baptized by the Rev. Mr. Titus Oates, and reared in the shadow of Newgate. His education is carefully calculated to produce a truly great prig. At school he directs all the depredations of his schoolmates, and shows no interest in any books except those which recount the histories of great plundering conquerors, such as Julius Caesar and Alexander of Macedon. Jonathan's schooling is further improved by the private tutoring of Count La Ruse, a famous gamester confined in Newgate for debt. This worthy gentleman recognizes Jonathan's genius and prepares him for entrance into the great world. Shortly after his debut the young man suddenly and unexpectedly takes the grand tour for seven years, but through His Majesty's colonies in America, not through Europe.[160] Upon his return he finds himself regarded as a great man, and, acting accordingly, begins to form a gang, of which he is to be the director.

Also an addition of Fielding's is the account of Wild's courtship of the beauteous and chaste Laetitia, daughter of Geoffrey Snap, a bailiff of Newgate. A match between the two had long been contemplated by their families, but the coy Laetitia chooses to test Jonathan's devotion by treating him badly. He finds particularly vexing her strategem of granting the freedom of her person to all admirers except himself. Finally the two are married and live in great harmony for a fortnight; then they fall out and live in complete domestic infelicity, like any couple in high-life.[161] They are confined in Newgate for different crimes at about the same time. Their final meeting occurs when Laetitia comes to upbraid her husband, who has just been sentenced, for dragging her into such disgrace. Jonathan takes his last leave of his wife by throwing her out of his cell.

Finally, Fielding introduced the Heartfrees, and made their conflict with Wild the chief matter of the second and third books of *Jonathan Wild.* Thomas Heartfree, an old schoolfellow of Wild's, is an honest, benevolent, and rather gullible jeweler. Wild renews acquaintance with him, and plots to rob him of his jewels and his beautiful wife, whose amiability Wild has misinterpreted as an invitation. The robbery is carried out, and Heartfree is taken up and committed to Newgate because some of the stolen jewels belonged to other dealers, who hope by confining Heartfree to secure themselves against loss. Wild, then, under the pretense of helping the afflicted family, begins to persecute them. He persuades Mrs. Heartfree to fly with him to Holland to safeguard what little remains of her husband's property. The ship is caught in a storm, and Wild, resolving not to allow possible shipwreck to prevent the fulfillment of his chief purpose, attempts to satisfy his lust by force. He is prevented by the captain, who puts him overboard in a small boat. Fortune returns him to London, where he begins to plot the utter ruin of Heartfree. After several unsuccessful attempts Wild manages to furnish enough false evidence to have Heartfree convicted of fraud and sentenced to be hanged. Heartfree lies in Newgate until the day appointed for his execution, when he is saved by a timely reprieve and happily reunited with Mrs. Heartfree. Meanwhile, Wild has been caught in his own stratagems, and has entered upon the final period of his career.

Obviously, Fielding was not interested in writing a conventional biography. Jonathan Wild is not the subject of an analytical study; he is the hero of an ironic narrative. In the Preface Fielding remarks: "To confess the Truth, my Narrative is rather of such Actions which he might have perform'd, or would, or should have perform'd, than what he really did. . . . Roguery, and not a Rogue, is my Subject."[162] In other words, Jonathan Wild interested Fielding because he was a personification of knavery.

For the Opposition writers Jonathan Wild was a symbol of political arbitrariness and corruption. It is well known that Fielding was associated with the Patriots. He was held by personal ties to Lord Lyttelton, and admired the political professions of Bolingbroke and Chesterfield. From the time of *The Beggar's Opera* and *Polly*, Fielding followed and occasionally contributed to the propaganda against Walpole, as indeed did most of the wits of the time. Beginning with *The Coffee-House Politician* and *The Tragedy of Tragedies*, Fielding devoted a great deal of dramatic energy to comedies, burlesques, and farces, which, in one way or another, attacked corruption and arbitrariness in government. With the genial *Don Quixote in England* and the caustic *Grub Street Opera, Pasquin,* and *Historical Register for the Year 1736,* Fielding, following John Gay, became the outstanding writer of political satire in dramatic form.[163]

After he was silenced by the Licensing Act in 1737, he began writing for *Common Sense*,[164] in which the criminal-politician parallel was fully exploited. One of the few essays in that journal definitely identified as Fielding's is a letter from "Pasquin," defending *The Beggar's Opera.*[165] In November, 1739, Fielding, having adopted the pseudonym "Captain Hercules Vinegar," became the chief writer of *The Champion* a thrice-weekly semi-political sheet modeled on *The Spectator.* His signed and unsigned articles in *The Champion* anticipate both the matter and the manner of *Jonathan Wild.*[166] In *The Champion* Fielding specifically refers to Jonathan Wild, using the name in the satirical manner made familiar by Opposition writers. One reference is in an essay on the lack of correspondence between virtue and good reputation, obviously a side-glance at Walpole. It reads: "Actions have sometimes been attended with Fame, which were undertaken in defiance of it. *Jonathan Wild* himself had for many years no small share of it in this Kingdom."[167] A second mention occurs in a somewhat later paper which, though not unquestionably written by Fielding, was probably his. A passage ridiculing the exultation of Walpole's adherents over the failure of the Parliamentary motion against him concludes:

But when we find all this stupid Subject of Triumph amounts to no more than what might full as well have befallen a *Jonathan Wild,* and the clamour made about it, little different from what might have been expected from his Confederates, it makes one smile. . . .[168]

These are Fielding's first direct references to Jonathan Wild.[169] They are both political in import. It was doubtless his knowledge of the satirical techniques employed by the Opposition writers that prompted Fielding to choose Jonathan Wild as the central character of his first long narrative—a work in which political satire is an important element.[170]

The political connotations of *Jonathan Wild* have long been recognized and have been elsewhere amply and ably discussed.[171] It has been pointed out that Wild is repeatedly called "the great man," a title which commonly directed attention to Sir Robert Walpole. In a manner made familiar by Patriot writers, the life of a great thief from birth to death is made parallel to the life of a Prime Minister. Fielding's general practice in *Jonathan Wild* is thus stated by J. E. Wells:

At practically every point of prominence where the matter concerns Wild, occur comment and application that are made by deliberate statement or by implication to point to persons in authority, particularly to those of political activity—to conquerors sometimes, but commonly to statesmen or ministers of state. Moreover . . . Wild is made active in passages ostentatiously political in their significance, when no such activity or significance properly belongs to Wild, or to the position in life of Wild as he is represented in the surface story proper.[172]

The effect of Fielding's political bias on his portrayal of the central character in *Jonathan Wild* is noteworthy. For political purposes Jonathan Wild becomes, like Walpole,[173] a composite of arbitrariness, corruption, hypocrisy, cruelty, and greed. When he was a schoolboy a sugarplum was more effective in assuring his good behavior than any number of threats. This susceptibility to bribery "made many say he was certainly born to be a Great Man."[174] Furthermore, he was the nonactive director of any project which involved profitable plunder of orchards and such, and kept his schoolfellows under his control by reporting recalcitrants to the master.[175]

In later life Wild similarly maintains rigorous control over his subordinates—Count La Ruse, the gamester; Bob Bagshot,[176] the street-robber; Fireblood, the desperate highwayman; Blueskin, and others. For example, after two hired bravoes, Sly and Fierce, rob the jeweler Heartfree, Wild, to protect himself, forces the pocket-picking harlot Molly Straddle to swear an information against Fierce. At Wild's suggestion Sly, a docile thief, offers evidence against Fierce, and the poor man is speedily condemned and hanged. Ironically, Fielding comments:

> With such infinite Address, did this truly GREAT MAN know how to play with the Passions of Men, and to set them at Variance with each other, and to work his own Purposes out of those Jealousies and Apprehensions, which he was wonderfully ready at creating, by Means of those great Arts, which the Vulgar call Treachery, Dissembling, Promising, Lying, Falsehood, &c., but which are by GREAT MEN summed up in the collective Name of Policy, or Politicks, or rather POLLITRICKS. . . .[177]

Jonathan Wild is prudent enough, however, to make a point of giving his actions the appearance of virtue. He introduces a speech in which he soothes the feelings of two gamesters, one of whom has accused the other of cheating, with a discourse on "Honour":

> [No Man can] possibly entertain a higher and nobler Sense of that Word, nor a greater Esteem of its inestimable Value than myself. . . . It is indeed, the essential Quality of a Gentleman, and which no Man who ever was great in the Field, or on the Road (as others express it) can possibly be without.[178]

Continuing, he defines "a Man of Honour" as "he that is called a Man of Honour. . . ."[179] The assembled company thereupon regards him as a good and wise man. Later, after he has organized a considerable gang, he observes among them a deplorable tendency to quarrel about the hats which they wear. Some wear fiercely cocked hats and some "nab," or "trencher," hats, and between the two factions there is constant animosity. Wild quiets this dissension in a masterful speech, which begins: "Gentlemen, I am ashamed to see

Men embarked in so GREAT and glorious an Undertaking, as that of robbing the Publick, so foolishly and weakly dissenting among themselves."[180] Hats, he says, are nothing in themselves; they merely amuse the mob and make the picking of pockets easier. It is skillful to pretend to quarrel, for that diverts suspicion. But "to be in earnest, and privately to keep up such a ridiculous Contention among yourselves, must argue the highest Folly and Absurdity."[181] Wild concludes with an exhortation to his thieves that they forget such differences and "consider that Hat as the best which will contain the largest Booty."[182] Substitute "principles" for "hats" and the satire becomes obvious. At the time of his death Jonathan put down as one of his maxims: "That Virtues, like precious stones, were easily counterfeited; that Counterfeits in both Cases adorned the Wearer equally, and that very few had Knowledge or Discernment sufficient to distinguish the counterfeit Jewel from the real."[183]

Although Jonathan Wild is careful to preserve the pose of virtue in public, he is not deceived by his own pretenses. In several soliloquies he candidly analyzes his system and reveals its essential selfishness. For example, when he is contemplating the formation of a gang, he divides the "superior" part of mankind into those who employ hands for the public good and those who employ hands for private gain. In the latter class he places conquerors, absolute princes, statesmen, and prigs. He asks himself rhetorically, "Now, suppose a *Prig* had as many Tools as any Prime Minister ever had, would he not be as great as any Prime Minister whatsoever?"[184] Since supremacy in the latter category of mankind is his ultimate desire, he asks:

What then have I to do, in the pursuit of Greatness, but to procure a Gang, and to make the Use of the Gang center in myself. This Gang shall rob for me only, receiving very moderate rewards for their Actions. . . . Out of this Gang I will prefer to my Favour the boldest and most iniquitous, as the vulgar express it; the Rest I will, from time to time, as I see Occasion, transport and hang at my Pleasure.[185]

This ruthless selfishness, reflective of the practices of the original Wild, was, as has been pointed out, the characteristic most often attributed to Walpole by the Opposition.

The action which most clearly reveals Jonathan Wild's political ability is that in which Wild, a newcomer in Newgate, successfully opposes and displaces Roger Johnson, the "very GREAT MAN, who had long been at the Head of all the Prigs in Newgate, and had raised Contributions on them."[186] Moved by a desire to have for himself the great power enjoyed by Johnson, Wild conducts a vigorous campaign against him, eloquently representing to the prisoners that Johnson has shamefully enslaved them, and promising to give them a free and honest government. All Newgate is split by the controversy. When the issue comes to a test, Wild's votes so outnumber Johnson's that the old leader yields. Then, to the dismay of his supporters, the new prime minister of Newgate promptly appropriates for his own use all of Johnson's insignia of office and becomes more insolent, autocratic, and insatiable than his predecessor. The debtors, most of whom had taken sides in this campaign, express their disaffection by uniting under the leadership of "a very grave Man" and separating themselves from all political association with the Prigs.

Considered in relation to the political events of 1741 and 1742, this is obviously an allegorical passage. Walpole is now represented by Roger Johnson; the election in Newgate symbolizes the Parliamentary elections of 1741, in which Walpole's majority, reduced to sixteen, was so uncertain that he resigned. The identification of Wild after this transformation is more difficult. W. L. Cross, drawing an analogy between *Jonathan Wild* and *The Beggar's Opera,* suggests that Wild, like Lockit, now represents Charles Townshend.[187] J. E. Wells believes that the victorious Jonathan stands for William Pulteney.[188] After Walpole's resignation, Pulteney, one of the original members of the Opposition, refused George II's invitation to form a new government. He did ask, however, to be named to the council, and recommended for posts in the cabinet several of Walpole's adherents. These compromises with the enemy made him unpopular with the Patriots.[189]

Perhaps a better candidate than either of these is John Carteret. Carteret, too, had for some time been associated with the Opposition. It was he who, on February 13, 1741, introduced in the House of Lords the motion urging the King to dismiss Walpole forever from his service, and supported it with an eloquent address. But when Walpole left the cabinet in February, 1742, Carteret gladly accepted the position of Secretary of State in the new government, which was made up largely of Walpole's men, and soon became virtually prime minister. For his conduct in office Carteret was in December, 1743, denounced by William Pitt, who was becoming the most prominent of the Patriots.[190] It is easy to see how Carteret, the renegade Patriot, might be as distasteful as Walpole to Fielding, who agreed with the genuinely nonpartisan Patriots in desiring the destruction not only of Walpole but also of the whole system of arbitrary and corrupt government which he represented.[191]

The unexpected substitution of another minister of state for Walpole as the butt of this satire is not extraordinary. Fielding himself says in his Preface that anyone acquainted with the "great world" could identify Jonathan Wild with each of several persons of quality.[192] Careful consistency, furthermore, was no part of the technique of Opposition satirists. In *The Beggar's Opera*, Walpole is represented by Peachum, by Macheath, and by Lockit. As a further complication, Lockit also represents Charles Townshend, the recalcitrant minister who left Walpole's cabinet in 1730.[193] Moreover, this shift in Jonathan Wild is indicative of a motivation much deeper than that provided by political partisanship. In 1752, some years after the strife which culminated in Walpole's fall, Fielding revised *Jonathan Wild* in such a manner that the actual attack on Walpole was much softened. But even this revision did not change the satiric core of the work. In the *Jonathan Wild* of 1743 Fielding was not primarily interested in defaming Walpole, Pulteney, Carteret, or any other single man. "Roguery," he announced in the Preface, "and not a Rogue, is my Subject. . . ."[194] He was in accord with those among the Patriot group who genuinely wished to see honest and public-spirited governors, no matter of what party, in control of England. He opposed Walpole because he regarded the Prime Minister as "the exemplar of the unjust glorification of perversion of political activity and of baseness and selfishness of personal life and ideal. . . ."[195] To an extent unusual among men of his time Fielding's political ideas and loyalties express fundamental moral convictions.

The political satire in *The Life of Mr. Jonathan Wild the Great,* therefore, must be considered as an aspect of the fundamental ethical problem—the conflict between "greatness" and "goodness"—to an examination of which the following pages are devoted.

CHAPTER TWO

THE ETHICAL PROBLEM

I N THE introductory chapter to *Jonathan Wild* Fielding offers his definition of terms: "Greatness," he assumes, "consists in bringing all Manner of Mischief on Mankind, and Goodness in removing it from them."[1] Here in an epigram is the statement of the ethical conflict which actuates Fielding's narrative of the life of Jonathan Wild.

The opposition between greatness and goodness is more carefully stated in the remarks on *Jonathan Wild* contained in the Preface to the *Miscellanies*. Having described the common confusion of goodness and greatness as "a Mistake of the Capacity for the Will," Fielding draws the following distinction:

In Reality, no Qualities can be more distinct: for as it cannot be doubted but that Benevolence, Honour, Honesty, & Charity make a good Man; and that Parts and Courage are the efficient Qualities of a Great Man, so must it be confessed, that the Ingredients which compose the former of these Characters, bear no Analogy to, nor Dependence on those which constitute the latter. A Man may therefore be Great without being Good, or Good without being Great.[2]

The opposition of these two qualities, Fielding adds, although common, is not essential. Goodness and greatness on rare occasions do blend in the same man to produce "the *true Sublime* in Human Nature." Simple goodness is inferior to this perfection "and yet hath its Merit." But simple goodness, no matter how unheroic, far excels unmodified greatness, which, says Fielding, resembles "the *False Sublime* in Poetry; whose Bombast is . . . often mistaken for solid Wit & Eloquence, whilst it is in Effect the very Reverse."[3] This spurious greatness, usually accompanied by riches and power and often by honor, is deceiving the world. Fielding, as a moral satirist, sets himself the task of exposing it and showing it "in its native Deformity."

Fielding did not invent the terms "greatness" and "goodness" or the meanings which he attached to them. The concepts represented by these two words as used in *Jonathan Wild* find frequent expression in the writings of early eighteenth-century moralists. The problem of greatness versus goodness was, as later discussion will demonstrate, merely one phase of the complex problem of the essential badness or goodness of man, the question which more than any other occupied ethical theorists of the Enlightenment. But the poets, essayists, and dramatists who wrote about greatness and goodness were for the most part but casually concerned with the total human significance of their writings. They were really concerned with delighting and instructing actual readers. Henry Fielding was such a writer; although deeply interested in moral philosophy and widely read in the ancient and modern sages, his attitude and purpose were nevertheless those of an intelligent and practical amateur who "bears his erudition like a gentleman." He filled his plays, poems, essays, and novels with his learning, expressed with a regard to the general capacity of his audience. In other words, Fielding, like Steele, Addison, Pope, and many another, was a popularizer. It is natural, therefore, that numerous expressions of the ethical concept basic to *Jonathan Wild* are to be found in the popular literature of the first forty years of the eighteenth century.

THE GREAT MAN: STATESMAN, CONQUEROR, OR ROGUE

Writers commonly translated the idea of greatness into the character of the "great man," whose attributes provided a basis for both straightforward and ironic moralizing. The great man found few defenders; the characteristics generally ascribed to him exposed him to vigorous condemnation. Occasionally the great man was conceded the possession of uncommon "parts." Henry Baker, for example, wrote: "A Great [Reputation] . . . is produced by Talents and Abilities, far above the common Standard. . . ."⁴ For the most part, however, writers neglected this single admirable quality and concentrated on the great man's essential viciousness.

However they phrased their abuse, they would have agreed that the prime characteristic of the great man is an immoderate, insatiable, and ruthless personal ambition. He is a man of action, not of thought; with the single exception of Machiavelli, the philosophical advocate of power does not rank as a great man. "Civicus" is fearful of "the bold ambitious Man, the restless turbulent Spirit, who must be great, cost what it may. . . ."⁵ "Cato" believes that great men "are . . . in the Wrong through Ambition, and continue in the Wrong through Malice."⁶ The writer of an essay "Of True and False Ambition" heartily condemns that "Ambition [which] tends to promote a personal Greatness which cannot consist with publick Safety."⁷ *The Whole Duty of Man,* during the late seventeenth and early eighteenth centuries a widely used handbook of morality, subjects ambition to a severe castigation: "Now Ambition is not only a great sin in itself, but it puts men upon many others. There is nothing so horrid, which a man that eagerly seeks greatness will stick at; lying, perjury, murder, or anything will down with him, if they seém to tend to his advancement. . . ."⁸ An anonymous essayist, commenting on the recently published *Discours sur le grand homme et l'homme illustré* of the Abbé de Saint-Pierre, cites as commonly accepted the view which identifies the great man and the powerful man.⁹ A similar point is made by an author writing "On Greatness" in *Mist's Weekly Journal.* He gloomily observes that a careful examination of history will reveal that the worst men, animated by ambition, have achieved fame in heroic exploits. Their success, he concludes, "authenticates the worst Cause, casts a Mist before our Eyes, and the Greatness of the Actions, from being too much admired, comes to be approved; as we often mention with Wonder the extensive conquests of the *Macedonian Youth,* but never condemn his unbounded and destructive Ambition."¹⁰

One of the most eloquent and vigorous discussions of the part played by ambition in the character of a great man is contained in an essay by Richard Steele. Using as his motto a quotation from Samuel Garth's *The Dispensary*—

> Little Villains must submit to Fate
> That great ones may enjoy the World in State—

Steele blames all the evils which beset mankind on ambition, which he defines as "the Desire of Preheminence, without Regard to the Means, whether just or unjust."[11] According to Steele, men who are moved by this passion have more regard for the applause of the many than for the censure of the thoughtful few. Despite the fame which great men easily achieve, they are the enemies of human-kind; to attain their ends they do not hesitate to ravage whole na-tions and slaughter whole peoples. The first ambitious man was Cain, and all who have followed him partake of his nature.[12] Of incalculable benefit to the world, Steele suggests, would be "a Genius great enough (accompanied with a Spirit sufficiently reso-lute) to put this Vice in a ridiculous Light. . . ."[13] One might well believe, from the ethical import of *Jonathan Wild,* that Fielding had read this essay in *The Englishman.*

The examination of greatness in popular literature was carried farther than this somewhat vague personification in terms of the great man. The great man was individualized, and regularly ap-peared as a politician, statesman, or courtier, as a tyrant or con-queror, and as a common rogue.

The representation of the great man as politician in the propa-ganda of the Opposition to Walpole has already been touched upon. The great man was Robert Walpole, who was characterized chiefly by his arbitrariness and corruption in government.[14] These qualities were manifestations of the personal ambition which, according to the Opposition, was Walpole's ruling passion.

The frequency of the portrayal of the great man as politician is suggested by "Humphrey Oldcastle's" remark: "The *great Man* is an Expression, which hath undoubtedly occasion'd more *Sneers* than this Nation hath seen in a Century before. . . ."[15] Greatness and vice were synonymous. In *The Statesman's Progress,* a parodying fusion of *Pilgrim's Progress* and *The Life and Death of Mr. Bad-man*, the statesman, having followed Truth a short way, grows weary and asks if there is not a less rugged way to "Greatness Hill," his goal. Truth answers that "Vice-Road" is much easier, but full of "People who had Regard neither for Honour or Conscience. . . ." Badman happily abandons the guidance of Truth and, placing himself under the protection of the Queen of Vice, rapidly gains the summit of "Greatness Hill."[16] Ambrose Philips, writing before Robert Walpole came into power, thought politicians generally vicious. In an early number of *The Free-Thinker,* having labeled statesmen "Great Men," he remarks: "The bursting of a Bomb in a Crowd is not more alarming, than the discharging of a Truth among modern Statesmen."[17] Several later papers deal with the iniquities of bad statesmen.[18] The series reaches a climax in an essay in which Philips condemns most ministers for being more concerned with the cabals of the court than with the debates of the council chamber. Statesmen in general, he declares, are little interested in the public welfare; they are characterized by "an insatiable Thirst of Power," and for them the highest enjoyment of this power is in abusing it.[19]

Heavy satire, similar to that found in *The Statesman's Progress,* pervades the number of *The Craftsman* in which Caleb D'Anvers first belabors the character and qualifications of the political great man—a subject of which writers for *The Craftsman* never tired. The essay begins with a generalization:

There is nothing, in which the Generality of Mankind are so apt to be mistaken, as in their Opinion of *Great Men.* They commonly judge by the outside; and where they see power, riches, and splendor, they hastily conclude, that there must be great parts and abilities in proportion: as for Honesty, it is quite out of the question, for even the vulgar herd know better than always to look for that qualification in a modern *Great Man.*[20]

Modern politicians become great, D'Anvers insists, chiefly by pimping, informing, stock-jobbing, and screening ministers and courtiers. He contrasts this shameful condition with conditions in former times, when integrity and ability were required of great men, and cites Sir Francis Walsingham and Lord Burleigh as examples.

Historical personages also furnished the Opposition writers with examples of the destructive activities of great men of the past. Machiavelli, as one might expect, is mentioned as a master among oppressive politicians.[21] Baron de Goerts (Georg Heinrich von Görtz), the German-Swedish diplomat who became principal adviser to King Charles XII of Sweden, is occasionally blamed for that spectacular monarch's fall.[22] Anti-Walpole writers found implied comparisons with great ministers of English history even more effective. A letter to Caleb D'Anvers, for example, analyzes the character of Cardinal Wolsey, as he appears in Shakespeare's *Henry VIII.* The political application is unmistakable.[23] Also mentioned are George Villiers, first Duke of Buckingham, Thomas Percy, Robert Dudley, Roger de Mortimer, and Thomas Osborne, Earl of Danby. Accounts of the official actions of these great men show" how court favorites and prime ministers misled the King, and misruled the people, and finally came to grief themselves."[24]

As a natural ally to the great man as politician appears the great man as tyrant or conqueror. Disturbed perhaps by the victories of Louis XIV of France and Charles XII of Sweden, popular moralists of the early eighteenth century began inquiring into the conduct of rulers. All princes came under a certain amount of suspicion, and those whose fame rested on military achievement alone became anathema.[25] Ambrose Philips asserts that overweening ambition is "the Vice to which Princes are mostly addicted,"[26] and, according to the Reverend Samuel Clarke, a disposition to tyranny is natural to most rulers.[27] Clarke again handles this theme in his sermon "The Great Duty of Universal Love and Charity," preached before the Queen on December 30, 1705. In speaking of conquerors he reaches a climax of denunciation:

To employ great power and riches in conquering and subduing many nations, in causelessly oppressing multitudes of people, and subverting the common rights and liberties of men; is the greatest folly, as well as the greatest wickedness imaginable; and nothing can be more weak and contrary to reason, than to call that ambition by the name of glory and greatness, which is really the most inglorious and dishonourable thing in nature.[28]

Richard Steele contributed to the general outcry against conquerors; the tyrant, he predicts, will disregard all territorial integrity and all treaties, and will not allow his forces to lay down their arms "'till all Men are reduced to the Necessity of hanging their Lives on his wayward Will."[29]

Even after Louis XIV and Charles XII had ceased to menace England, the censure of conquerors was a moral commonplace. An anonymous vindicator of the fundamental goodness of mankind blames all *"national or general Evils"* of history on great men, particularly "tyrannical princes and wicked priests."[30] A writer for *The Craftsman* shares this opinion, labeling the great conquerors of the past *"Imperial Cut-throats or Banditti."*[31] Thomas Secker, Archbishop of Canterbury, asserts that the heart of a tyrant, habituated "to executions and slaughter by long use," must be harder than the heart of any other wicked man.[32] The literature of the period abounds in examples, similar to these, of the disapproval with which popular moralists of the early eighteenth century regarded over-ambitious rulers.[33]

A pointed example fortifies any general conclusion, and detractors of tyrants and conquerors accordingly singled out one or another for censure, until few such great men had escaped a belaboring. The four most frequently chosen were Alexander the Great and Julius Caesar—universally considered the most famous conquerors of antiquity—and Louis XIV of France and Charles XII of Sweden—regarded during the early part of the eighteenth century as the most fearful threats to the peace and security of England and the continent. It was generally agreed that Alexander had been "very falsely and unjustly celebrated for his heroick virtue."[34] The Macedonian's traditional jealousy of Achilles and his supposed chagrin upon finding no new worlds to conquer were often cited as evidence of his vicious and destructive ambition.[35] Boileau in 1663 launched a poetical thunderbolt at Alexander. Having observed that ambition is always the ruling passion of so-called heroes, the French satirist continues:

> Quoi donc? à vostre avis, fut-ce un fou qu'Alexandre?
> Qui? cet écervelé qui mit l'Asie en cendre?
> Ce fougueux l'Angeli qui de sang altéré,
> Maistre du monde entier, s'y trouvoit trop serré?
> L'enragé qu'il estoit, né Roi d'une province,
> Qu'il pouvoit gouverneur en bon et sage prince,
> S'en alla follement, et pensant estre Dieu,
> Courir comme un Bandit qui n'a ni feu ni lieu,
> Et traînant avec soi les horreurs de la guerre,
> De sa vaste folie empli toute la terre.[36]

Mandeville and Pope followed Boileau's lead and dubbed Alexander "Macedonia's Madman."[37] Pope's remarks on the greatness of conquerors are worth quoting:

> Look next on Greatness: say where Greatness lies.
> 'Where but among the heroes and the wise?'
> Heroes are much the same, the point's agreed,
> From Macedonia's madman to the Swede;
> The whole strange purpose of their lives to find,
> Or make, an enemy of all mankind.[38]

Caesar was frequently mentioned as an inferior imitator of Alexander, whose victories the Roman bitterly envied.[39] Although his force of arms was awesome, he had to rely heavily on extravagant bribery to maintain his position.[40] Caesar did, to be sure, increase the power of Rome, but he minded only his own interest.[41]

The two contemporary rulers, Louis XIV and Charles XII, achieved reputations as monstrous as those of their ancient counterparts. Steele, masking as "Philarithmus," lamented the vanity of conquests. As his prime example he chose the French king, "generally esteemed the greatest Conquerour of our Age," and damned him for causing the death of thousands of innocents.[42] Several years earlier, Nicholas Rowe, in his tragedy *Tamerlane* (1702), had panegyrized William III as the noble Tamerlane and defamed Louis

XIV as his monstrous antagonist, Bajazet. Bajazet is obviously a
great man. His activating principle is expressed in these lines:

> Can a King want a Cause, when Empire bids
> Go on? What is he born for, but Ambition?
> It is his Hunger, 'tis his Call of Nature,
> The Noble Appetite which will be satisfy'd,
> And like the Food of Gods, makes him immortal.[43]

As a personality Charles XII was more spectacular and terrifying
than Louis XIV. From earliest youth the Swedish king cherished a
desire to become the preëminent warrior of his time. To that end,
according to Voltaire, "full of the idea of *Alexander* and *Caesar*, he
proposed to imitate these two conquerors in everything but their
vices."[44] After displacing the regents and crowning himself king in
1697, Charles began a cyclonic career of conquest. He quickly subdued Denmark, Poland, and Saxony. In 1707 he invaded Russia;
after preliminary successes he was overwhelmingly defeated at Pultowa in 1709. After five fruitless years spent in soliciting Turkish
aid, Charles returned to Sweden, his empire depleted but his spirit
undaunted. He unwisely undertook to regain part of his power
by invading Norway and threatening Scotland. He was killed in
1718 while his forces were besieging an unimportant Norwegian
fort.

The character of Charles provided a text for several moralists. In
1714 Bernard Mandeville commented with great bitterness upon
the zeal with which Charles XII was ruining his kingdom.[45] Posthumous commentators were severe but understanding. A certain
Mr. Van Essen, author of *A Relation of a Journey from Holland
into Sweden*, blamed Charles's dazzling faults on a vicious education, praised the sovereign's energy and endurance, and exonerated
him from charges of cruelty and inhumanity.[46] Voltaire, whose
detailed and circumstantial biography was very popular in England,[47] grants Charles many virtues, but concludes that it was "his
failing to drive all the virtues to excess." Voltaire's final characterization of his subject is a mixture of censure and forbearance:

Perhaps he was the only man, to be sure he was the only King, who ever had lived without weakness. . . . His great qualities, any one of which had been enough to make another Prince immortal, were a misfortune to his country. . . . He was the first who ever had the ambition to be a conqueror, without wishing to encrease his dominions. His desire to gain Kingdoms was only that he might give them away. The passion he had for glory, for war, and for revenge, made him too little of a politician, without which the world never saw before any Prince become a conqueror. . . . [He was] a man extraordinary rather than a great man, and fitter to be admired than imitated. His life, however, may be a lesson to kings, and teach them that a peaceful and happy Government is more to be desired than so much glory."[48]

The general character of Charles XII was well known in England. Voltaire's biography, translated into English soon after it appeared, had a wide circulation, and has remained a classic life of the Swedish king. Pope's reference to Charles XII has already been noted. Even more famous are the lines in which Samuel Johnson points to the Swedish monarch as an example of the vanity of "warrior's pride." Beginning bravely, "a frame of adamant, a soul of fire," he had but a brief period of glory. "His fall," the passage concludes,

> was destined to a barren strand,
> A petty fortress, and a dubious hand;
> He left a name, at which the world grew pale,
> To point a moral, or adorn a tale.[49]

Tyrants and conquerors, either historical or fictional, proved particularly useful to the Opposition writers who were sponsored by the Patriots. These writers—notably James Thomson, Richard Glover, David Mallet, and Henry Brooke— took as a statement of faith Lord Bolingbroke's *Letter on the Spirit of Patriotism* (1736).[50] Toward the beginning of this work Bolingbroke postulates that the "Author of Nature" sees fit to bestow extraordinary capacities on certain men, who are born to guide, preserve, and instruct mankind. "When these men," the noble lord continues, "apply their talents to other purposes, when they strive to be great, and despise being good, they commit a most sacrilegious breach of trust."[51] As if to illustrate this pronouncement, two Patriot dramas,

Mallet's *Mustapha* (1739) and Brooke's *Gustavus Vasa* (1739),[52] contain characters who are intent on being great at the expense of goodness.[53] In *Mustapha* Solyman, the Turkish emperor, is led by his wife and two evil counselors, Rustan and Mufti, to mistrust Mustapha, his devoted and noble son. The "lawless monarch" is so blinded by suspicion that he destroys a princely son who would certainly have developed into a "Patriot King." Brooke's *Gustavus Vasa,* the performance of which was forbidden by the licenser, provides even better examples of the dramatic use of the great statesman. The action represents the successful revolt of Gustavus Vasa against the tyrant Cristiern, king of Denmark and Norway, and usurper of the throne of Sweden.[54] Cristiern is portrayed as a great man. Speaking to Trollio, his vicegerent, he proclaims:

> Yes, *Trollio,* I confess the Godlike Thirst,
> Ambition, that would drink a Sea of Glory.[55]

A little later in the same dialogue he reveals more fully his oppressive political philosophy:

> Kings should be felt if they wou'd find Obedience;
> The Beast has sense enough to know his Rider,
> When the Knee trembles, and the Hand grows slack,
> He casts for Liberty; but bends and turns
> For him that leaps with Boldness on his Back,
> And spurs him to the Bit.[56]

Assisted by his Machiavellian minister Trollio, Cristiern throws all his might against the patriotic and benevolent Gustavus Vasa. The tyrant's forces are completely routed; Cristiern kills Trollio for his false and misleading counsel, and goes mad from disappointment over the loss of his Scandinavian empire.[57] Solyman and Cristiern are both ambitious monarchs, men of extraordinary capacity, whose passion for greatness overcomes their goodness.[58]

The great man as common rogue has been discussed previously in connection with the use of Jonathan Wild's name and reputation by Opposition satirists.[59] The great man and the rogue were, however, identified by many writers who could have had no desire to dislodge Walpole from office.[60] In 1698 Boileau, still crusading against the worship of false heroes, asserts:

> Un injuste Guerrier, terreur de l'Univers,
> Qui sans sujet courant chez cent Peuples divers,
> S'en va, tout ravager jusqu'aux rives du Ganges,
> N'est qu'un plus grand Voleur que Dutarte et Saint Ange.[61]

In a note he identifies Dutarte and Saint Ange as "fameux voleurs de grand chemin." Steele professes to respect the felons—"great Men in their Way"—whose actions are recorded in Captain Alexander Smith's *Complete History of the Lives . . . of the Most Notorious Highwaymen . . .* more than the "far greater Criminals, who are described with Praise by more eminent Writers."[62] Similarly, the rogues who swindled the nation in the South Sea Bubble are said to deserve hanging as much as the little rogues who pick private pockets.[63] In another instance a satirical biographer of one of the South Sea directors thus acknowledges his debt to Captain Alexander Smith, his "Master in *Biography*": "He wrote only the Lives of little Rogues, I of great Ones. . . . He has however this Advantage over me, that his Heroes are generally Men of better Spirit, gentiler Education, greater Courage, nobler Endowment, and, very often, much better descended than mine."[64]

On his third voyage Swift's Gulliver visited Glubbdubdrib, the island whose inhabitants were conversant with spirits, and acquainted himself with the famous dead. He viewed the Senate of Rome and its modern counterpart. The one seemed to him "an assembly of heroes and demi-gods"; the other resembled "a knot of pedlars, pickpockets, highway-men, and bullies."[65] Gulliver's feeling about the heroes and venerable personages of modern history was one of disgust. He saw only cowards, fools, flatterers, atheists, informers, whores, pimps, and rogues of all kinds. They freely confessed "perjury, oppression, subornation, fraud, and panderism;" these were their lesser crimes. Some "owed their greatness and wealth to sodomy or incest, to the prostituting of their own wives and daughters; others to the betraying their country or their prince; some to poisoning, more to the perverting of justice in order to destroy the innocent."[66] These were the great men of their time; the word *criminal*, Swift implies, is scarcely damning enough for them.[67]

As politician, as conqueror or tyrant, and as common rogue, the great man was thus exposed to the condemnation and scorn of poets, essayists, and dramatists, whose aim was the moral instruction of their readers. Because of the Opposition's insistence on the greatness of Walpole, there is a temptation to attach to the terms "greatness" and "great man" a solely political connotation. This is a misplacing of emphasis. The basic idea of greatness—the quality which "consists in bringing all Manner of Mischief on Mankind"—was a moral commonplace during the first half of the eighteenth century. The political writers merely employed it more often and more effectively than did writers who lacked a definite target.

THE GOOD MAN

It is hardly necessary to demonstrate, moreover, that goodness—the active force, which, according to Fielding, removes from mankind the evil done by greatness—was the prime concern of many popular writers of the early eighteenth century. From the beginning of his literary career Defoe was seldom without a moral purpose. *The Tatler, The Spectator,* and *The Guardian,* whose influence on journalistic practice remained strong almost to the end of the century, were avowedly devoted to the improvement of manners and morals. These are but two of the most obvious examples; ethical didacticism permeated not only the literature of purpose, but belles lettres as well.[68]

In order to impart to morality a simple, common-sense appearance, goodness was personified in the good man—frequently a Sir Roger, a Parson Adams, a Sir Charles Grandison, or a Dr. Primrose, occasionally just "the good man."[69] Charles Whittuck found this model person to be characterized chiefly by completeness of personality, by the coöperation within him of religion and virtue, and by fortitude in withstanding—and even profiting by—suffering.[70] A contemporary "Character of a good Man" partially bears out Whittuck's conclusions. In sum, according to this essay, the good man is an orthodox Christian and a true lover of his country. He is guilty of no excess, except perhaps of charity; he is tender, but not raw, of conscience. A well-balanced man in every respect, his company is delightful to all men of sense.[71]

Of the many incarnations in which the good man appeared, two are important here—the good man in politics and the good man in history. Early eighteenth-century writers on statecraft laid great emphasis on the necessity for moral uprightness in political activity,[72] and freely censured the practicing politicians who disregarded this principle.

In opposition to selfishness and arbitrariness—in more familiar terms, to greatness—moralists urged "Publick Spirit" and patriotism. "Publick Spirit," in the words of Edward Bentham, is a "settled and reasonable principle of Benevolence to, or hearty concern for the welfare of human Society."[73] An anonymous writer defined "Publick Spirit" as simply "Good Nature"—a term virtually synonymous with goodness—"widely diffused."[74] Patriotism, closely related to "Publick Spirit," is, according to Bentham, "an intire uniform love of our Country."[75] This author immediately adds, however, that patriotism is peculiarly the concern of "men of publick stations."[76] This view was indeed the common one, and the good man in politics regularly occupies a position of authority. Samuel Clarke in a sermon entitled "The Character of a Good Man" states that as magistrate or governor the good man "will take much more pleasure in being able to be publickly beneficial to mankind . . . than in obtaining to himself power, for power's sake."[77] The implied denunciation of political greatness is unmistakable. An unselfish goodness is required even of a ruler. In David Mallet's *Mustapha* Zanger, the loyal half brother of the hero, proclaims:

> A Prince's life is not his own:
> Not for himself, he lives for the human race.
> This universal duty to your Kind
> Cancels all private bonds.[78]

A few speeches later Mustapha states his belief that a monarch should be "Heaven's true Vicegerent," whose goodness and beneficence far exceed in genuine glory the "tyrant's selfish prowess."[79] Mallet's tragedy was, of course, intended as a dramatization of the ideals of the Patriot party. Disinterested love of country was the first principle of this group of Walpole's enemies. Bolingbroke's *Letter on the Spirit of Patriotism* and *The Idea of a Patriot King* begin with the thesis that unimpeachable virtue, superior wisdom, and self-abnegating love of country are the essential qualities of the "Patriot King." This monarch must always act on the assumption that "the ultimate end of all governments is the good of the people."[80] Kings who lack the initial perfection which Bolingbroke demands fall into evil from two causes: their own vanity and the machinations of artful, self-interested men.[81] One can detect censure of Walpole beneath these fine sentiments. The Patriot writers were skilled in adapting to their purposes and language and ideas of non-partisan political moralists. The good man in politics proved very useful to the Patriots and other members of the Opposition, but he was not their invention.

The good man of history is usually introduced in implied or expressed contrast to some great man. Cincinnatus, the humble, incorruptible Roman patriot, is opposed to Pericles, the irresponsible Athenian ruler.[82] Throughout Voltaire's life of Charles XII, the king of Sweden and the czar of Russia, Peter I, are weighed in the balance, always to the advantage of the latter. Peter is thus honored because he applied his genius for organization and command to good government and the internal improvement of his country, and not, as did Charles, to vain conquest.[83] Voltaire phrases the contrast more pointedly in his introduction to his biography of Peter I: "On juge aujourd'hui que Charles XII méritait être le premier soldat de Pierre-le-Grand. L'un n'a laissé que des ruines; l'autre est un fondateur en tout genre. . . . L'histoire de Charles XII était amusante; celle de Pierre Iᵉʳ est instructive."[84] The other great men—tyrants and conquerors—whose eighteenth-century reputations were examined a few pages previously were also contrasted with the good men of history. Alexander, in the opinion of an anonymous moralist, "had no commendable motive, since he acted only for his own interest and advancement."[85] Consequently, the virtuous and patriotic Theban general Epaminondas, although far inferior to Alexander as a soldier, must be considered the better man. Caesar's selfish, tyrannical ambitions render him less admirable than Scipio Africanus Minor, who "settled the inward and outward Liberty of the Republic and added to the power of *Rome* the whole power of Carthage."[86] Likewise, the assassin Brutus's worth, purely as a man, far excels his victim's.[87]

Toward the beginning of the eighteenth century loyal English writers, particularly Whigs, delighted in drawing a sharp contrast between Louis XIV and William III.[88] Steele devotes a considerable section of *The Christian Hero* to a vigorous comparison between a tyrant and a benevolent king. Although Steele uses no names, it is obvious that his two rulers are Louis XIV and William III. Contrasting these personages was one of Rowe's objectives in *Tamerlane*. The fiendish Bajazet represents the French king, while the triumphant and benevolent Tamerlane stands for the English sovereign. Rowe underlines the latter identification in his dedication: "His [Tamerlane's] Courage, his Piety, his Moderation, his Justice, and his Fatherly Love of his People, but above all his Hate of Tyranny and of Oppression, and his zealous Care for the common Good of Mankind, carry a large Resemblance to him [William III]...."[89]

This panegyric of King William might serve as an epitome of the praise bestowed by ethical writers of the early eighteenth century on the good man of history. Obviously this virtuous personage has a kinship with the Patriot, as he is characterized in Bolingbroke's *Letter on the Spirit of Patriotism* and in other pronouncements of the coterie surrounding that noble lord. But the good man of history, like the political good man to whom he is related, is not the original property of the Patriot group. The concept of the good man and his several personifications are moral commonplaces of the times.[90]

SELF-LOVE AND BENEVOLENCE

The conflict between greatness and goodness found in the literature of popular morality has its parallel in the learned speculation of the time. In general, formal ethics of the late seventeenth and early eighteenth centuries converged upon the problem of the essential nature of man and his fitness for society. The crucial concepts—and terms—were "self-love" and "benevolence." Is man actuated primarily by a vicious self-interest or by a disinterested and friendly disposition toward all rational agents? Is self-love itself a vice, or does it become so only when present to excess? Can self-love and benevolence coëxist, and, if properly balanced, contribute to the well-being of the individual? Such questions as these held the attention of English ethical theorists from Thomas Hobbes to Joseph Butler. To be sure, a great intellectual distance separates the philosophical inquiry into the nature of man from the journalistic, dramatic, or poetical sermon on greatness or goodness. But the two are related. The one is an immediately disinterested search for unsimplified truth; the other, a simplified piece of moral propaganda, written to influence an unlearned audience. The one concerns abstract ethics; the other, conduct. A closer examination will reveal more clearly the relation of the greatness-goodness opposition to the basic problem of formal ethics, which can best be considered in terms of self-love and benevolence.

In the ethics of Thomas Hobbes the fundamental characteristic of man is his selfishness. All natural human action springs from a self-love which is more likely to be aggressive and acquisitive than tenacious. In Hobbes's own words: "in the first place, I put for a general inclination of all mankind, a perpetual and restless desire of power after power, that ceaseth only in death."[91] The important thing about this inherent lust for power is that it is insatiable. Hobbes continually emphasizes this idea of human dynamism. Because "life itself is but motion," he says, there can be no tranquillity or satisfaction. Human felicity consists in *continual success* in obtaining those things which a man from time to time desireth, that is to say continual prospering. . . ."[92] In another passage he states that "to have no desire is to be dead"; in still another he makes happiness depend on "a continual progress of the desire." Perhaps Hobbes's most forceful statement of this concept occurs in his essay "Human Nature, or the Fundamental Elements of Policy," which makes up the first part of *Tripos* (1640). In a strategically placed passage he says:

Seeing all *delight* is *appetite,* and presupposeth a *further* end, there can be *no contentment* but in proceeding: and therefore we are not to marvel, when we see that as men attain to more riches, honour, or other power; so their appetite continually groweth more and more; and when they are come to the utmost degree of some kind of power, they pursue some other, as long as in any kind they think themselves behind any other. . . . *Felicity,* therefore, by which we mean continual delight, consisteth not in *having* prospered, but in *prospering.*[93]

A condition of life in which every man pursues felicity in this fashion cannot be a peaceful and orderly one. Competition between man and man is literally deadly; ruthless force and fraud are the best devices both for defense and offense. Such a state, Hobbes believes, would be the inevitable result if every man followed his natural inclination unchecked. The state of nature is a state of war. Law and order can be introduced into such a world only if a strong authority forces every man to make a contract foregoing some of his natural lust for power in return for a safe, peaceful life. But the constituted authority must keep the contract in force by coercion, for man's essential irrational desire is only subdued, never eradicated.

There is an unmistakable similarity between natural man, as conceived by Hobbes, and the great man of the popular moralists. Both are moved primarily by an inordinate self-love, which expresses itself in excessive ambition,[94] and in aggression unrestrained by compassion for fellow beings or concern for social good. Neither of them is satisfied with the gains of a limited conquest; their lust for power "ceaseth only in death." There is a difference between them in that the natural man is the normal occurrence in a pre-societal state, whereas the great man is a prodigious occurrence in a state of civilization. This difference does not, however, alter the fact of their spiritual kinship.

Most ethical theorists after Hobbes, disciples and opponents alike, agreed that self-love is a fundamental passion and that an excess of it is a great cause of human evil-doing. Bernard Mandeville lays down as a first principle that "all untaught Animals [including man] are only solicitious of pleasing themselves . . . without considering the good or harm that from their being pleased will accrue to others."[95] In order to make his basic paradox—"private vices, public benefits"—the more startling, Mandeville professes to regard as vicious any act motivated by self-love. By this standard the bees in their prosperous hive and, by inference, men in productive society are entirely vicious.[96]

Even the more kindly and optimistic thinkers—Richard Cumberland, Benjamin Whichcote, the Earl of Shaftesbury, Francis Hutcheson, Joseph Butler, and others—who in determined opposition to Hobbism defended man's essential goodness and benevolence, could not deny the occurrence of a self-love which is excessive and destructive. Shaftesbury sees in man three types of affections: those which interest him in the public good; those which interest him in his own well-being; and those which interest him in neither. The first two types are perfectly natural, while the third is not. The problem of right living, and hence of happiness, is a problem of keeping the public and private affections in proper balance. The guide in this constant process is an intuitive moral sense. A man who is oversupplied with the selfish affections "beyond their degree of subordinacy to the kindly" is both vicious and miserable. The height of evil and misery is produced by the operation of the third type, the unnatural affections; but these, significantly enough, are frequently nothing more than greatly exaggerated manifestations of self-interest.[97] Hutcheson likewise finds the ordinary springs of vicious action in "mistaken self-love."[98] Bishop Butler thinks the distinguishing intellectual and moral characteristic of his time to be "a contracted spirit, and greater regard to self-interest."[99] This spirit he considers the very foundation of evil. "Vice in general," he says, "consists in having an unreasonable and too great regard to ourselves, in comparison to others."[100]

The ethical theorists discussed here—both Hobbesians and anti-Hobbesians—probably could not have agreed upon a precise and formal definition of self-love. It is safe to assume, however, that the term carried much the same general and informal meaning for all of them. Bishop Butler stated it simply and clearly, "Every man hath a general desire of his own happiness. . . . [This] proceeds from, or is, self-love; and seems inseparable from all sensible creatures, who can reflect upon themselves and their own interest or happiness."[101] The disagreement between the two groups came over the degree to which the passion is present in untutored and uncontrolled man. Hobbes emphasized man's lust for power. Since man lacks a native capacity for social wisdom and virtue, he must be forcibly kept in his place.[102] The anti-Hobbesians believed, first, that man's essential selfishness is by no means so thoughtless and aggressive as Hobbes states, and, second, that it is nicely balanced by an equally strong, or stronger, benevolence toward all fellow-creatures. Hobbes virtually identifies *amour de soi* and *amour propre;* the benevolists distinguish between them.

Benevolence, the affection which the anti-Hobbesians consistently opposed to unrestrained self-love, is easier to apprehend than to define. In general, it was conceived as a fundamental tendency which impelled man to be amiably disposed toward his fellow-man and actively to seek his happiness. Hume asserts that "the character of the good and benevolent" is composed of generosity, humanity, compassion, gratitude, friendship, fidelity, zeal, disinterestedness, and liberality[103]—terms which certainly overlap. According to R. S. Crane, who believes that the real fountainhead of benevolism is to be found in the writings and pronouncements of late seventeenth-century Latitudinarian divines, "the words 'charity' and 'benevolence' had a double sense, connoting not only the serviceable and philanthropic actions which the good man performs, but still more the tender passions and affections which prompt to these actions and constitute their immediate reward."[104] He also considers that the most important effect of the liberal preachers' doctrine "was the dissemination of the idea that man is essentially a gentle and sympathetic creature, naturally inclined to society, not merely by his intellect . . . but still more by 'those passions and inclinations that are common to him with other creatures.'"[105] This emphasis on man's disinterested goodness to others had, of course, been anticipated by Hobbes. As might be expected, he had made benevolence simply a disguised operation of the desire for power. He says, "There can be no greater argument to a man of his own power, than to find himself able not only to accomplish his own desires, but also to *assist* other men in theirs. . . ."[106]

The benevolists wisely made no attempt to deny Hobbes's first principle; they sought rather to absorb it. Self-love they recognized as a natural, necessary, and even virtuous motivation, but not the sole one. Private affections and public reside in every man's breast; the problem of morality is the problem of keeping the two in proper balance. When equilibrium is maintained, the two principles assist each other and bring to the virtuous possessor the highest felicity possible in this world. Occasionally, an ambitious man, by allowing self-interest to overbalance his inherent benevolence, achieves a success so spectacular that it seems superhuman. Such fortune, however, is always impermanent; the strong and constant disapprobation of conscience soon makes the man revolt against himself, and true inner happiness deserts him.[107] Joseph Butler gave perhaps the most effective answer to Hobbes. The Bishop distinguished between genuine self-love and the mere gratification of passion or appetite. He judged self-love by its ultimate, not its immediate, result. Any self-interested action which produces eventual unhappiness because of the disapprobation of the all-regulating conscience is not genuine, but false, self-love. True self-love and benevolence coöperate perfectly, and both are subservient to the highest principle—conscience.[108]

The essential notion of the benevolists is epitomized in the familiar words of Alexander Pope, the man who more than any other popularized their doctrine for the intelligent and fashionable laity:

> Thus God and Nature link'd the gen'ral frame,
> And bade Self-love and Social be the same.

The correspondence between the controversy over self-love and benevolence and the greatness-goodness opposition is by no means an exact one. Writers of popular expositions simplified the terminology and the arguments and virtually ignored the philosophical modifications. This difference, however, does not alter the fact that goodness approximates pure benevolence and greatness unrestrained and aggressive self-love. Even on the level of politics, journalism, and polite conversation, according to C. A. Moore, "The moral question at issue between these two systems of philosophy— the egoistic and the benevolent—became soon after the publication of the *Fable* [*of the Bees*] the most absorbing topic of public discussion."[109]

FIELDING AS MORALIST

Fielding's writings before *Jonathan Wild* clearly reveal that their author was preöccupied with the moral questions then current. For a number of reasons, chiefly Fielding's own belittlement of his work and the misrepresentations of Arthur Murphy, readers have been slow to recognize the earnestness of many of the early essays, poems, and theatrical pieces. Admittedly some of this work can never be regarded as better than scribbling. Nevertheless, the best of Fielding's early efforts contain emphatic forecastings of that large-souled morality which invests and elevates the great novels.

Fielding the playwright, journalist, and poet was much concerned with the greatness of popular morality. The early works are filled with references to it, some of which amount to informal definitions. Greatness is the basic and motivating trait of a number of characters in the plays. Indeed, the great man, as politician, conqueror, or rogue, finds more prominence in Fielding's early works than in the works of any other writer of the time. Goodness receives not so much direct attention, but enough to make it a topic of almost equal importance. In short, the ethical content of Fielding's early work centers on the contest between greatness and goodness. An examination of Fielding's unsystematized observations on this subject necessarily precedes a study of the moral basis of *Jonathan Wild* itself.

In his portrayal of the great man as politician, Fielding does not notably depart from the common satiric practice of the time. The great statesman minds his own interest exclusively, to the detriment of the state's. Not wisdom and patriotism, but lying, impudence, and ingratitude are the virtues most necessary for succeeding in politics,[110] and bribery is the politician's most useful device for gaining his ends. In *Pasquin* Lord Place and Colonel Promise, the "court" candidates, are shown bribing the mayor and his aldermen. Fustian, the tragic author, asks, "Is there nothing but bribery in this play of yours, Mr. Trapwit?" The answer is pat: "Sir, this play is an exact representation of nature."[111] Immediately Sir Harry and the Squire, "the country" candidates, enter and diligently secure the same votes, less openly but just as unscrupulously as did their rivals. *The Historical Register* concludes with a scene in which Quidam bribes four false Patriots to dance for him. As they caper about, the money falls from their pockets and rolls back to its master.[112] In *The Vernoniad,* an elaborately annotated burlesque epic poem, Mammon bribes Aeolus himself to turn the winds against the six ships of the heroic Admiral Vernon, so that he will be prevented from taking Porto Bello.[113]

Quidam and Mammon, of course, represent Robert Walpole. Enough has already been written about Fielding's attacks on the Prime Minister.[114] It should be emphasized, however, that Fielding did not subordinate his convictions to political partisanship. The election scenes in *Don Quixote in England* and *Pasquin* and some passages even in *The Historical Register,* the entertainment which provoked the Licensing Act, condemn not merely the sins of the Walpole government but political malpractice in general. Undoubtedly Fielding was drawn both for personal and professional reasons to the Opposition. Nevertheless, a contempt for narrow self-interest was part of his fundamental moral attitude, and he assailed political greatness wherever he saw it.

If Fielding despised the great statesman, he hated conquerors and tyrants, the false heroes of history, as if they were alive and active. To him they are robbers and murderers, who, motivated by sheer ill nature, have "imposed severe Laws, invented cruel Punishments . . . sent abroad Fire and Sword and Faggot, to ravage, burn, depopulate and enslave Nations."[115] Fielding spends little time in analyzing the abstract character of this kind of great man. Ambition, vanity, strength, and cruelty—all present in excess and mingled in a uniquely vicious composite—form the character of the tyrant or conqueror.[116] As Fielding writes about him, he ceases to be a man and becomes almost a symbol of the evil which results when the fundamental selfishness of man runs unrestricted. Fielding's sense of truth was further outraged by the tendency, observable in certain historians, to make heroes of these—the worst of men. This false exaltation is attacked, not only in many straightforward essays, but also in burlesque works, notably *The Tragedy of Tragedies; or The Life and Death of Tom Thumb the Great.* Fielding's general target in *Tom Thumb* is heroic tragedy, as written by Dryden, Banks, Lee, and others. Specifically he makes sport of their bombastic language and their unnatural and exaggerated characters.[117] Underneath Fielding's ridicule, however, lies a serious disapproval of the heroic presentation of wicked men.

Alexander the Great came under Fielding's particular displeasure. Alexander is "that Madman . . . who disdain'd any Father but Jupiter."[118] In "A Dialogue between Alexander the Great and Diogenes the Cynic" Alexander boasts to his detractor of the slaughter and rapine for which he has been responsible:

Thou dost speak vainly in Contempt of a Power which no other Man yet arrived at. Hath the *Granicus* yet recovered the bloody Colour with which I contaminated its Waves? Are not the Fields of Issus and Artela still white with human Bones? . . . Have not the Groans of those Millions reached thy Ears, who but for the Valour of this Heart and the Strength of this Arm, had still enjoyed Life and Tranquillity?[119]

In the moral epistle "Of True Greatness" Fielding brands both Alexander and Julius Caesar as universal enemies and contrasts them with the late Duke of Marlborough as a warrior whose purpose was not the mad destruction of mankind.

Of the other conquerors and tyrants who suffer an occasional denunciation, Charles XII of Sweden deserves some notice here. It seems beyond doubt that Fielding, in the capacity of a "hackney-writer," translated from the French Gustavus Adlerfeld's *Military History of Charles XII, King of Sweden*.[120] This work is an "official" account of Charles's career up to the time of the battle of Pultowa; his exploits are admiringly rehearsed in great detail, with unconscious emphasis on the devastation caused by his campaigns. The moral standard implicit in this work doubtless annoyed Fielding as much as that in *Pamela,* and a reaction against praising the Swedish conqueror probably fortified his already vigorous anti-heroism.[121]

As a text for Fielding's treatment of the great man as common rogue, a passage in the fourth issue of *The Champion* might be selected:

The World, says *Montaigne,* are cheated with the Appearances of Things, not the Realities. . . . We may carry this Observation pretty safely thro' all of our Opinions of Things. What we look on as Power, Honour, Wisdom, Piety, &c. are often not the Things themselves, but the Appearances only.[122]

The sight of a rogue occupying a high place, doing his will without fear of retribution while lesser rogues suffered disproportionately, never failed to anger Fielding. Villainy to him was villainy, and the guilty one deserved exposure and punishment, no matter what his position and pretensions. Whether he was writing about literature, history, politics, or human conduct, Fielding crusaded against affectation and hypocrisy. Actually he regarded any great man—statesman, tyrant, or conqueror—as an exalted hypocrite, who must be exposed in the light, not of his reputation, but of his true character. In "An Essay on the Knowledge of the Character of Men" he warns against trusting the "Flatterer," the "Professor," the "Promiser," or *soi-disant* "Censor," and argues that the undisguised actions of men provide the only reliable key to their natures.[123] *The Modern Husband,* perhaps Fielding's most serious play, ends with the unmasking of Mr. and Mrs. Modern, Lord Richly, and other sinners in high life. *The Coffee-House Politician* is in part devoted to the discovery and deposing of Justice Squeezum, a corrupt magistrate who administers punishment according to the station of the guilty one.[124]

Indeed, the logical corollary of Fielding's enmity toward hypocrisy is his contempt for the justice which hangs the poor pickpocket and frees the much guiltier noble lord. In *Eurydice* Mr. Spindle, meeting Captain Weazel in hell, asks to be introduced to the devil as one who was hanged. The captain hastily admonishes him. Only poor rogues, he says, are hanged; if you wish to be welcomed "tell him you deserved to be hanged, but was too great for the law."[125] In another play Don Quixote, obviously speaking for Henry Fielding, summarizes the matter thus:

Sancho, I am not concerned at the evil opinion of men....Look through the world. What is it recommends men but the poverty, the vice, and the misery of others? This, Sancho, they are sensible of: and therefore, instead of endeavouring to make himself better, each man endeavours to make his neighbour worse. Each man rises to admiration by treading on mankind. Riches and power accrue to the one by the destruction of thousands. These are the general objects of the good opinion of men.... I'm not mad enough to court their approbation.[126]

The fact that Swift, Pope, Gay, and others had made the vices of high-life a common theme of social satire detracts from the originality of Fielding's attacks on the roguery of the "right honourable," but not from their sincerity. His hatred of greatness and of the great man was a matter of temperament.[127]

In opposition to greatness Fielding lays emphasis on "good-nature," which he considers "Virtue's Self."[128] He defines this quality frequently; perhaps the best single statement is this:

Good-Nature is that benevolent and amiable Temper of Mind which disposes us to feel the Misfortunes and enjoy the Happiness of others;

and consequently pushes us on to promote the latter, and prevent the former; and that without any abstract Contemplation on the Beauty of Virtue, and without the Allurement or Terrors of Religion.[129]

Fielding expends a great deal of literary effort in urging the merits of good-nature, which has everything to recommend it. It demands no harsh self-denial, only temperance and moderation. It is in no way inconsistent with a reasonable attention to self-interest; indeed, the practice of good-nature furthers private well-being.[130] Whereas greatness requires the exertion of the violent competitive passions, good-nature is far less assertive. Consequently, the good-natured man does not suffer from the vexations and disappointments which beset the great man. Good-nature offers in place of the dubious pleasures of greatness the permanent joy which comes from the consciousness of virtue.[131] Fielding's good-nature, in short, is nothing more than a simplified, informal, common-sense version of the elaborate doctrine of benevolism. Fielding has been so often presented as the robust, realistic satirist, the scorner of all cant, that it is easy to forget the softer side of his nature.

This brief recapitulation of the ethical content of Fielding's early work should demonstrate that before writing *Jonathan Wild* Fielding partially formulated his concepts of greatness and goodness. Although he had frequently contrasted the two he had not brought them into definite and complicated conflict. In *Jonathan Wild* Fielding personified these abstractions—greatness in Wild and goodness in Thomas Heartfree and family—and presented the ethical contest in narrative form.

Using his earlier ideas on greatness as a base, Fielding in *Jonathan Wild* evolved an expanded and more conscious theory of greatness, which represents an individualized expression of the ideas commonly found in the works of the popular moralists. Frequently throughout *Jonathan Wild* the action is interrupted by sentences, paragraphs, and whole chapters of comment on the nature of greatness. A long dialogue between the Count La Ruse and young Jonathan Wild makes the now familiar point that the same abilities compose the statesman, the conqueror, and the prig. "The same

Parts," the philosophizing Wild remarks, "the same Actions, often promote Men to the Head of superior Societies, which raise them to the Head of lower; and where is the essential Difference if the one ends on *Tower-Hill* and the other at *Tyburn?*"[132] Sometime after this conversation Wild, finding himself restless, begins to meditate on ways and means of attaining greatness. He considers mankind as properly divided into two classes: "those that use their Hands, and those who employ Hands." Of the second division, "the genteel Part of Creation," there are those who employ hands for the general good and those who employ hands for their own use and advantage. In the latter group belong "*Conquerors, absolute Princes, Prime Ministers,* and *Prigs.*" The degree of greatness depends solely on the number of hands employed. Alexander was greater than one of his captains only because he headed a larger force of men. A prig would be as great as a prime minister if he had as many tools. Accordingly, Wild determines to assemble a gang which will rob for him and which he will control by judicious hanging and transporting.[133] With this resolution begins his ascent to real greatness.

In such passages as the foregoing Fielding, frequently using Wild himself as a mouthpiece, expounds a theory according to which greatness is essentially a vicious and destructive principle of individual men which operates to the detriment of all men. His many expositions of this principle,[134] some of them elaborate, can be reduced to his own simple, inclusive definitions, "Greatness consists in bringing all Manner of Mischief on Mankind,"[135] a statement which agrees with the general conclusions of the popular moralists. Greatness as an idea, however, has little didactic force when separated from its human manifestations. Accordingly, Fielding, who always put more faith in example than in precept, embodies greatness in a character who epitomizes the principle.

Jonathan Wild, as portrayed by Fielding, achieved a greatness unparalleled in history or romance. His ruling passion was an insatiable ambition which robbed him of complacence, and, indeed, of happiness. Nothing ever satisfied him but the whole. "The truest Mark of GREATNESS," Fielding remarks, "is Insatiability."[136] Wild was not content to plunder Heartfree of all his jewels and plunge him into ruin; he did his utmost to debauch the man's wife and to send him to the gallows. For the pursuit of greatness nature had endowed Wild with many gifts, all of which he had assiduously fostered and improved. He was consummately bold, cunning, and resolute. Reverses of fortune stimulated him to greater efforts. His all-absorbing self-interest enabled him without a pause for thought to deal ruthlessly not only with his victims but with his underlings as well. A dangerous or rebellious "Prig" speedily found his way to the gallows. Wild was further aided in dealing with men by his extraordinary ability to make capital of another's weakness. He knew the good Heartfree to be gullible and easily imposed upon. During most of his campaign to ruin and hang the jeweler Wild kept his victim's esteem simply by pretended services and extravagant professions of friendship. This genuis for hypocrisy was the talent which Wild most valued in himself and in others. Although he held good-nature and good actions in contempt, he carefully cultivated an affectation of virtue and modesty, and relied on this appearance to serve him as well as, or better than, the reality. Indeed, one of the maxims which he left for the instruction of others who might aspire to greatness was: "That Virtues, like precious Stones, were easily counterfeited; that Counterfeits in both Cases adorned the Wearer equally, and that very few had Knowledge or Discernment sufficient to distinguish the counterfeit Jewel from the real."[137]

Wild lacked the weaknesses which would encumber a man seeking greatness. The word "honesty" he believed to be a corruption of the Greek word for an ass.[138] Modesty and good-nature he had always avoided as qualities which "implied a total Negative of human GREATNESS." Although his lust was tremendous, he was incapable of entertaining the tender passion which simple people called love, either for a woman or for mankind in general. His feeling toward all human creatures except himself was a composite of contempt, suspicion, and hatred. Like Alexander and Caesar he never in his life performed an act of genuine benevolence. Occasionally, of course, Wild lapsed into weakness; he felt a severe twinge of remorse when the dead warrant came for the innocent Heartfree. These feelings, however, were few and momentary, and did not really detract from his consummate lack of virtue.

With such a character it is little wonder that Wild's life was a triumph of greatness. Certain heroes and conquerors, "who have impoverished, pillaged, sacked, burnt, and destroyed the Countries and Cities of their fellow Creatures, from no other Provocation than that of Glory,"[139] may have perpetrated more widespread destruction, but none could have outdone Wild in his own province. He set himself arbitrarily over a gang of felons, ruled them with a tyrant's will, and through them, in open defiance of all law, plundered the commonwealth. "Indeed," concludes his historian, "while GREATNESS consists in Power, Pride, Insolence, and doing Mischief to Mankind;—to speak out,—while a GREAT Man and a GREAT Rogue are Synonymous Terms, so long shall *Wild* stand unrivalled on the Pinacle of GREATNESS. Nor must we omit here, as the finishing of his Character . . . that *Jonathan Wild the Great* was, what so few GREAT Men are, though all in Propriety ought to be—hanged by the Neck 'till he was dead."[140]

Thomas Heartfree, Wild's principal victim, offered a complete contrast to the great man. His dominating traits of character were good-nature and innocence. The former made him well disposed toward all the world—friend and stranger, rich man and poor man, Christian and Turk.[141] It also made him careless of his own interest. Heartfree never took advantage of his customers' ignorance of jewels; he had been known to forgive his acquaintances' debts, simply because they were unable to pay them. His innocence, which resulted not from simplicity but from good-nature, made him easy prey for the great man. Because of a grateful liking carried over from their long past school days, Heartfree admitted the apparently openhearted and friendly Wild first to his home and then to his confidence, without once suspecting that the great man's professions and intentions might not be the same. Not until Wild had repeatedly abused and deceived him did Heartfree begin to see the truth. Indeed, Heartfree, like most good-natured men, seemed "sent into the World by Nature, with the same Design as Men put little Fish into a Pike-Pond, in order to be devoured by that voracious Water-Hero."[142]

Just as Wild lacked any of the tender feelings of goodness, Heartfree lacked any of the violent passions of greatness. Desire for gain was perhaps the weakest motive in him. When persecuted he did not retaliate with violent resentment and reprisal. His only defense against Wild was a steadfast adherence to his virtuous principles, fortified by the conviction that, despite adversity, his conscience accused him of nothing. His lack of self-love made him content with a tranquil domestic life. Heartfree was well pleased to live in simple retirement with his wife, "a mean-spirited, poor, domestic, low-bred Animal, who confined herself mostly to the Care of her Family, placed her Happiness in her Husband and her Children; followed no expensive Fashions or Diversions, and indeed rarely went abroad...."[143] In the married state the Heartfrees were quite as peaceful and contented as Wild and his wife Laetitia, a great and fashionable lady, were quarrelsome and uneasy.

Heartfree is plainly related to the good man of eighteenth-century popular moralists. Fielding may, however, have received suggestions for his character from two other sources—the personality of George Lillo, a jeweler and a dramatist, and the literary presentation of the worthy merchant as a type character. Heartfree and Lillo are linked by a tradition of long standing. It is a commonplace that Fielding occasionally more or less modeled characters, particularly admirable ones, on actual persons; Parson Adams was drawn from the Reverend William Young, Sophia Western and Amelia from Charlotte Craddock,[144] and Squire Allworthy from Ralph Allen. There is, furthermore, evidence to suggest that Fielding held Lillo in considerable esteem. In 1736, as manager of the Haymarket Theatre, he took up Lillo's domestic tragedy *The Fatal Curiosity*, wrote a prologue for it, advertised it widely, and gave it an excellent production. The next winter he ran it as an afterpiece to *The Historical Register*. This bill proved highly successful.[145] When Lillo died in 1739, shortly before the production of his drama *Elmerick;*

or, Justice Triumphant, Fielding devoted an essay to his memory. He treated the new tragedy handsomely, and praised its author in a panegyric which, even allowing for the exaggeration of eulogy, bears witness to his high opinion:

> He had the Spirit of an old *Roman,* joined to the Innocence of a primitive Christian; he was content with his little State in Life, in which his excellent Temper of Mind, gave him an Happiness beyond the Power of Riches, and it was necessary for his Friends to have a sharp Insight into his Want of their Services, as well as good Inclinations or Abilities to serve him. In short, he was one of the best of Men, and those who knew him best, will most regret his Loss.[146]

Certain phrases in this appraisal might be applied to Heartfree. It probably cannot be proved that Fielding's character embodies or adumbrates the jeweler-dramatist, but the conjecture remains interesting and illuminating.

It seems, further, more than coincidence that Fielding made his good man a tradesman at a time when the worth of trade and of merchants was being discovered by politicians, men of letters, and the nonmercantile world in general. Commerce, both domestic and foreign, came to be regarded during this period as the source of England's wealth and power; the coming of the merchant, said his advocates, banished poverty and backwardness, and introduced prosperity and civilization. Such praise, the more vehement because of the traditional upper-class disdain for trade and tradesmen, can be found in Defoe's works on trade—*The Complete English Tradesman, A Plan of the English Commerce, A General History of Trade*—and in the mercantile rhapsodies of Glover, Young, Thomson, Dyer, Savage, and others.[147]

The tradesman, who in Restoration drama had served chiefly as a butt for jokes, became a respected character, possessed of dignity and virtue. Fairbanks, the goldsmith, in George Farquhar's *The Twin Rivals* (1702) is distinguished by his kindness to the deserving and hard-pressed elder brother. Sir Andrew Freeport of *The Spectator,* Mr. Sealand of *The Conscious Lovers,* and the Dutch merchant of *Roxana,* all command respect. Robinson Crusoe himself is a tradesman as well as a sailor; he draws up inventories and balance sheets, keeps a journal, and generally follows the habits of his calling even on the island.[148] Thorowgood, the employer of George Barnwell in *The London Merchant,* possesses all the virtues in the superlative degree. Even Hogarth's "Industrious Apprentice" represents a kind of "folk-hero of the first half of the eighteenth century."[149]

Two of these worthies, Crusoe and Thorowgood, deserve further mention. The cardinal virtues for a merchant were thought to be prudence, honesty, diligence, moderation, sobriety, and thrift. The young Crusoe's chief failing was a lack of prudence. The hardships of castaway life and the necessity of conquering the wilderness develop these virtues in Crusoe, so that by the time he leaves the island he possesses them all in full measure.[150] Thorowgood has all the admirable traits of Defoe's ideal merchants, plus one—kindliness. He will not entertain any proposals for the hand of his daughter Maria until he finds where her preference lies. To his good apprentice, Trueman, he is the best of masters. Even Barnwell, though an embezzler and a murderer, draws his compassion, not his condemnation. Thorowgood, furthermore, is given to extolling with tempered but unmistakable pride the excellence of trade and tradesmen. Honest merchants frequently "contribute to the safety of their country, as they do at all times to its happiness."[151] The name of merchant, Thorowgood believes, does not degrade the gentleman. Commerce "is founded in reason and the nature of things . . . it has promoted humanity . . . [and] arts, industry, peace, and plenty, by mutual benefits diffusing mutual love from pole to pole."[152] *The London Merchant* played for twenty nights to crowded houses and was frequently revived. Thorowgood and Trueman established the worthy merchant as a literary tradition.[153]

Fielding's attitude toward the dignification of the "middle class" in general and merchants in particular was undoubtedly favorable. That much can be inferred from his disdain for heroic themes and characters in drama, from his censorious treatment of fashionable society, and from his sympathetic portrayal of socially unpretentious characters—Parson Adams, Mr. Wilson, and others.[154] More specifically, he encouraged the performance of domestic tragedy during his managership of the Haymarket Theatre. He patronized Lillo, the chief writer of the new genre, and later Edward Moore, one of Lillo's successors.[155] In one of the first numbers of *The Champion,* Fielding ridicules excessive pride in lineage, wonders how such notions "crept into a Nation, whose Strength and Support is Trade," and expresses the belief that a man who brings money into his country by "a beneficial Trade" is as honorable as any aristocrat.[156]

Heartfree possesses the mercantile virtues of honesty, diligence, moderation, sobriety, and thrift; like Crusoe he is somewhat lacking in prudence. This failing, however, is the result not of stupidity but of his fundamental good-nature. In respect of this virtue Heartfree greatly resembles Lillo's Thorowgood; even his treatment of the devoted apprentice Friendly is the same as Thorowgood's. It would be extreme to say that Heartfree is intended to represent nothing but an admirable tradesman. Fielding was primarily concerned in portraying good-nature, which has never been the sole property of any social class. Nevertheless, it is likely that, led by his respect for George Lillo and his work, Fielding was influenced in his presentation of Heartfree by the literary tradition of the worthy merchant.

Wild and Heartfree are too highly simplified and invested with purpose to be completely lifelike characters. Wild is almost unremittingly great. Only when the dead warrant comes for the victimized Heartfree does he show any sign of compassion, and this brief yielding to weakness is banished by the reassertion of greatness.[157] Here and in other passages Fielding affects to excuse Wild by saying that complete greatness, or diabolism, is beyond the capacity of mere mortals. These apologies, however, are only another expression of his generally ironic attitude toward his central character. Wild is occasionally hindered in the pursuit of greatness by misfortune, fear, or fraud, but never by real goodness.

Heartfree is even less complicated than Wild. No suspicion of selfishness or ill nature taints the goodness of his character. He will not even strike back at his persecutor, for he conducts himself always according to a rule "OF DOING NO OTHER PERSON AN INJURY FROM ANY MOTIVE OR ON ANY CONSIDERATION WHATEVER."[158] Encouraged by Friendly, the apprentice, Heartfree does, to be sure, get out a warrant against Wild. But when the great man frees himself with the aid of a henchman's perjury, Heartfree lets the matter drop and goes quietly back to prison. In short, Wild and Heartfree are not so much characters as moral symbols. Heartfree's saintliness and capacity for suffering are hardly human; Wild's unrelenting persecution of the Heartfrees cannot be rationalized. Fielding is concerned with exposing and condemning greatness by contrasting it with goodness. He increases the effectiveness of this contrast by presenting it in an extreme manner. The characters in whom the opposing forces are personified, therefore, are necessarily uncomplicated and distinguished for a single trait.

Even though a symbol, Wild is more positive and individual than his victim. It is more than coincidence that he is the only person in the book who does not bear an allegorical name. This discrepancy between the main characters was undoubtedly intentional. Wild represents positive, active evil; Heartfree, negative, passive good. Wild is the attacker, Heartfree the attacked. That Fielding recognized this difference is shown by his statement that Heartfree's "Character . . . will serve as a kind of Foil to the noble and GREAT Disposition of our Hero . . . the one seems sent to this World as a proper Object on which the GREAT Talents of the other were to be displayed with a proper and just Success."[159] It is for this reason that throughout the action Heartfree seems, in comparison with the spectacular Wild, a weak, pale, and uninteresting character.

At first sight this discrepancy between the central characters may seem to indicate Fielding's lack of vital interest in goodness. But Fielding's chief purpose is to expose and condemn greatness, not to defend goodness, which wants not Fielding to support it. Goodness is simply one of his weapons against greatness; contrast itself becomes an ethical device.

During his career Fielding had much to say about active benevolence—about "doing good." He was not, however, unaware of the worth of simply "being good." In an early essay in *The Champion*, for example, he declares virtue, which he compares with nature, to be modest and unassertive, while vice, like art, is pretentious and noisy.[180] His heroine Amelia overcomes her husband's wildness by passive and unconquerable goodness. Similarly Heartfree distinguishes himself not by "doing good" but by "being good."

This fundamental difference between Wild and Heartfree is clearly reflected in their actions. Wild never rests; he is constantly planning or executing some villainous scheme. Although the ruin of Heartfree is his grand purpose, its fulfillment demands by no means all his energy and cunning. He vigorously carries on his regular business and neglects no venture which promises profit. By his unrestrained pursuit of greatness Wild actually works his own ruin. Like a tyrant or conqueror he carries his passion for self-aggrandizement to such an excess that it finally destroys him. The immediate instrument of Wild's destruction is Fireblood, the "second-rate Great Man" who is his trusted lieutenant. Fireblood proves as dangerous to Wild as an ambitious favorite to a prime minister. Fireblood secures enough information to impeach his master and to prepare the way for an inescapable indictment. Fireblood, however, is no more than an instrument. Even before he appears the reader knows that Wild is destined for the gallows. Greatness, Fielding implies, is an active force which brings destruction not only to its victims but also to its possessor.

Heartfree's passive goodness is his preservation. Against Wild's constant attacks, Heartfree defends himself with simple fortitude. Except for one abortive attempt he eschews active resistance and relies on a sort of Christian stoicism. When the dead warrant comes Wild's triumph seems almost complete. Actually it is not; Heartfree's consciousness of his own innocence gives him a serenity which is not disturbed even by the prospect of a disgraceful death at Tyburn. Greatness can never overcome the self-approbation which is the last refuge of goodness. But as Wild was destined for destruction, so Heartfree was destined for good fortune. With the revelation of Wild's guilt Heartfree's innocence is established. His wife returns from the wanderings which began when the lustful Wild abducted her, and brings with her the stolen jewels. The whole family is reunited in love and prosperity, and returns to a life of uninterrupted domestic tranquillity.[161] With this final demonstration of the superiority of simple, passive, goodness over aggressive greatness, the contrast is completed.

To summarize, popular writers of the first half of the eighteenth century, intent on the moral instruction and improvement of their readers, presented under varying names two opposing conceptions —greatness and goodness—which were simplifications of the ethical dualism on which learned speculation centered. Henry Fielding, a competent amateur in philosophy, adopted these popular notions, and in early essays, poems, and dramas developed them, giving particular attention to greatness, into well-defined theories. In *Jonathan Wild* he embodied greatness and goodness in radically contrasting characters and brought them into conflict. Ethically considered, then, *Jonathan Wild* is a popular allegorical presentation of a fundamental moral problem.

CHAPTER THREE

LITERARY FORMS AND TRADITIONS

THE HISTORICAL events and intellectual traditions which provided the materials for *Jonathan Wild* were shaped by Fielding to his own purpose, and the content of this work represents, therefore, an individual interpretation of preëxisting data. So much for the matter. Similarly, the manner of *Jonathan Wild* reveals traces of well-established literary forms and traditions —conventions which Fielding transmuted into an expression which is largely his own.

REALISM AND LOW-LIFE

Fielding labels *Jonathan Wild* the history of the life of a great rogue, thereby placing it in the tradition of English criminal biography. This genre had long been a flourishing one. Receiving their first impulse from the low-life sketches of Nashe, Greene, Dekker, Deloney, and others, anonymous authors of the seventeenth century supplied an eager and ungenteel public with accounts of pickpockets, footpads, highwaymen, swindlers, pirates, ruffians, and unworthies of all kinds and degrees. Any rogue, particularly one who had recently been brought to justice, furnished excellent material. Gamaliel Ratsey, William Longbeard, Long Meg of Westminster, Moll Cutpurse, James Hind, Richard Hainam, and Claude DuVall were only the most notorious of many chapbook and penny-pamphlet heroes.[1]

During the early part of the eighteenth century the volume of criminal biography increased. Each felon who was hanged became the subject, not of a single life, but of several, the number depending on his notoriety.[2] These rival lives were hawked to the crowd on the morning of execution. It is not accidental that a hawker occupies a conspicuous place in Hogarth's representation of the idle apprentice's progress to Tyburn. Such persons made an important part of the riotous scene on every hanging day. Indeed, competition among criminal biographers was so keen that the ordinary of Newgate, who was licensed by law to sell for his own profit the last dying speech and confession of each condemned malefactor, frequently had to defend his perquisite by releasing his account well before the execution.[3]

The vogue of criminal biography evoked a noteworthy censure from men who regarded such avid interest as both disgusting and dangerous. Swift wrote his revolting "Last Speech and Dying Words of Ebenezer Elliston ..."[4] to give the lie to accounts which romanticized criminals. Aaron Hill reviewed the whole subject of making capital of condemned malefactors, and concluded with an outburst against their biographers:

The Scribbler, the Pamphleteer, and the *Biographer of Newgate* . . . draw out his [the criminal's] good Name, and quarter it; and hang up his Reputation, in *Effigie*. They give him a *Quarto*, or an *Octavo* Shrowd; and fringe and flourish it with his *Birth* and *Parentage*. . . . If the Sufferer can write, and read, then, besides his *Birth*, and *Education*, his *Tryal* and *Confession*, we have his *Last Works* and *Compositions*. If he is married, we have his Widow's Lamentations. If he dies, troubled and unsatisfied, we have *his Ghost*. . . .[5]

The popularity and influence of criminal biography are indicated by the severity of these and other attacks[6] on its practitioners.

As might be expected of so occasional and unliterary a type, few conventions characterized eighteenth-century criminal biography. Those few, however, were carefully observed and are at once apparent. Because such lives were usually written to appeal to an intense but evanescent public curiosity, they were short, simple, and sensational. It was no part of the author's purpose to present a truthful account of his subject. Generally the outline of the rogue's life was followed with reasonable accuracy; within that outline, however, sober fact frequently yielded to lurid fiction.[7] Nevertheless, writers of criminal biography vigorously protested in title pages, dedications, and prefaces the genuineness of their products. Defoe, who as John Applebee's chief writer probably excelled all his competitors in reporting criminal news, frequently introduced his account of a rogue with a warning against the falsity and actual perniciousness of all other sources.[8]

Claims of authenticity were fortified by the realism and circumstantiality of the works themselves. Full details of birth, parentage, education, and early employment; an explanation of the subject's first venture in crime; names of confederates, particularly the notorious ones; rehearsal of his matrimonial and amorous adventures, with special attention to sordid entanglements; detailed narratives of his principal crimes, with names of the victims; a record of his previous arrests and punishments, or acquittals and escapes; an account of his final apprehension and trial, with any of his witty or solemn sayings on that or any other occasion; and a frequently too-vivid description of his manner of swinging out of the world—these were the components of the usual criminal biography. Half of these details usually represented the author's embellishments of fact; occasionally they were quite fantastic. "Captain" Alexander Smith, author of the first extensive collection of rogue biographies, assures his readers that Sir John Falstaff behaved gallantly against the Yorkists, and received a pension of 400 marks a year. Since this was not enough to support his "exorbitant licentiousness," the knight began robbing on the highway. His daring, in incidents cited by Smith, eclipses the most extravagant claims of Shakespeare's fat rogue.[9] It is hard to believe that Smith expected to gain his readers' complete credence; nevertheless, the fullness and straightforwardness with which he rehearses his tall tales suggest that he was intent on giving them at least a superficial aspect of truth. Such confident copiousness, much like that which enabled *The Journal of the Plague Year* to pass as history, generally characterizes rogue biography.

Another device of the Newgate biographer was to represent his work as the condemned man's confession and repentance.[10] Defoe's second life of Jack Sheppard, the manuscript of which he publicly received from Sheppard's own hands on the morning of execution,[11] purports to be a "full revelation." Written in an exclamatory first person, it rehearses all Sheppard's misdeeds and concludes with a canting appeal for the prayers of his readers. Not only did this confessional trick lend authenticity—it also gave a proper moral tone to the piece. Disguising sensational material with edifying reflections was a general practice in popular literature of the early eighteenth century,[12] and in no form was this device more common than in rogue biography. For example, "The Life of Joseph Blake, *alias* Blueskin," opens with this pronouncement: "He ... thought Wickedness the greatest Achievement, and studiously took the Paths of Infamy to be famous."[13] During the remainder of the sketch solemn declarations of the author's abhorrence balance exciting accounts of Blueskin's villainous adventures. Likewise, Defoe in his life of Jonathan Wild rarely misses an opportunity to express detestation of his subject's character and way of life. Such moral pretensions probably did not lessen or sober the reader's thrills, but Newgate biographers seldom omitted them.

Sometimes this moralistic approach was replaced by a satirical attitude, as in the jeering, abusive verses which appeared after Jonathan Wild's death.[14] The favorite device consisted in representing the departed as a hero, and in bestowing ironic praises on his valor, wisdom, and magnanimity, and on the glory of his exploits. In a "Dialogue between Julius Caesar and Jack Sheppard," which appeared in *The British Journal* for December 4, 1725, the recently hanged felon successfully defends himself against Caesar's taunts and makes him admit that "I have been as excellent in my way, as you in yours, perhaps more so."[15] Objective lives of criminals are rare; abhorrence is regularly expressed, either in straightforward moral condemnation or in satire.

In brief, then, eighteenth-century criminal biographies were characterized by brevity, fabrication, circumstantial realism, luridness, and moral pretentiousness or satire. Admittedly, they had few of the excellences of conventional biography. The characterizations of criminals contained in them were violent, but stereotyped; their subjects were invariably incarnations of vice. Their sketch of the criminal's social milieu was always the same. The pattern on which they were constructed was conventional to the point of monotony. Nevertheless, criminal biography should not go unheeded. In the hands of Defoe, who memorialized the Cartoucheans of France, Captain Avery, John Gow, and Duncan Campbell, it represented admirable reporting. In a period when most narrative was cast in a biographical mould, it helped impress on fiction a much needed realism.[16]

Criminal biography was, of course, one expression of a marked tendency in early eighteenth-century literature toward the artistic use of materials from low-life. Certain aspects of the tradition represented by the work of Tom Brown, Ned Ward, Peter Motteux, Roger L'Estrange, "Captain" John Stevens, and later of Defoe, Gay, Henry Carey, and others, are therefore relevant to a study of *Jonathan Wild*.

The literature of blackguardism made familiar to a sizable public all manner of raffish characters who haunted the streets, taverns, night cellars, and gaols of the metropolis. *The London Spy* takes its readers on a systematic tour of London, with special attention to the seamy side. Whores, thugs, beggars, bullies, quacks, rowdy soldiers and seamen, constables, and various other kinds of rascals swarm through the pages of this handbook of the town. In *Trivia* Gay carefully warns his readers against the many dangerous habitués of the streets, particularly those who walk by night. The dramatis personae of *The Prison-Breaker, The Quaker's Opera,* and *The Beggar's Opera* read like the combined rosters of Newgate, Bridewell, and the Mint.

For the most part, these low-life sketches offer little real characterization of the rascals whom they introduce. A constable is always greedy for bribes; bullies do nothing but roar and play cruel jokes; the gamester cheats continually. The characters of Defoe's biographical narratives of low-life offer a happy improvement over this stereotyped characterization. Moll Flanders, Colonel Jack, and Roxana cannot be called complex psychological studies, but as characters they are at least individually motivated.[17] Although born in Newgate and forced by poverty into a career of successful crime, Moll is haunted by her own conscience. At heart she remains a good woman, and her steadfastness is finally rewarded with a life of peace and comfort. Colonel Jack, during his painful rise from squalor to wealth, is guided by the knowledge that he is a gentleman born and by the conviction that he must remain worthy of his birth. Most of Roxana's adventures spring from a jealous desire to preserve her freedom and independence. It might almost be said that the central figures in Defoe's tales operate according to a ruling passion. Attention to realistic characterization, not notable in the works of previous narrative writers, constitutes one of Defoe's important gifts to English prose fiction.[18]

Defoe's characters do not, however, merit the term "low-life" so much as do some of his social settings, which are generally presented with that convincing exactness at which he excelled. These revealed to contemporary readers not only the physical aspects of Newgate, Bridewell, the Old Bailey, and the penal colonies in America, but also the manners and morals of the inhabitants of such places. Defoe's account of the squalid surroundings in which Colonel Jack spent his childhood and of his thieving, snatching companions gives a good insight into the conditions which helped produce enough desperate criminals to make London during the early part of the eighteenth century one of the most lawless and dangerous places in the world. The description of Newgate during Moll Flanders' imprisonment depicts a house of horrors—all kinds, degrees, and ages of offenders herded together; everyone, including the ordinary himself, drunk; thieving, extortion, and murder commonly practiced; starvation, disease, madness, and death everywhere. Defoe had seen what he was describing, and did not spare his readers' sensibilities.

Gay's famous low-life setting, although lacking the offensive detail of Defoe's, is none the less vivid. *The Beggar's Opera* imitates with great accuracy not only the manners and morals, but even the canting language of Newgate, the thief-taker's establishment, and the surrounding resorts of felons, bailiffs, and doxies. A complete society is represented. Actuated by greed, its members spend their lives robbing and cheating, but never get rich. Peachum demands all their booty and rewards them meagerly. The constant uneasiness of living in fear of want and the gallows instills in them a cynical gaiety which finds expression in their talk and in their songs. Peachum, the thief-taker, holds absolute power over his gang. He regards men merely as instruments for his own use, and pursues his own interest in a manner which is as cruel as it is efficient. Such is the social milieu presented in *The Beggar's Opera;* the best testimony to its verisimilitude is the ever-recurring suspicion that Gay himself was not quite a "respectable" person.

Another reason for the difference between Defoe's picture of the Newgate environment and Gay's lies in the fact that *The Beggar's Opera* is filled with satire aimed at the political great man, an aspect of the work already discussed. The presence of satire in *The Beggar's Opera,* however, is not entirely the result of Gay's personal bent, nor of his political purpose. The roguish society in *The Beggar's Opera* is a disreputable replica of high-life.[19] Just as a sneering attitude toward the subject is to be found in certain criminal biographies, so anti-heroical satire is common in early eighteenth-century literature of low-life.

This feature is admirably illustrated in Christopher Bullock's comedy *A Woman's Revenge; or, A Match in Newgate* (1715), an adaptation of John Marston's *The Dutch Curtezan.*[20] Vizard, "a notorious Cheat," interrupts the action occasionally to elaborate on his theory that all men, high and low, are rogues, moved solely by their own interest, and that the punishment of them depends upon position, not upon guilt. Vizard excels at the cynical *bon mot.* He defines friendship, for example, as "a Shadow that attends the Sun of our Prosperity."[21] The speech which virtually summarizes Vizard's opinions deserves full quotation, for its similarity to some of Fielding's dramatic discourses on the same subject:

Few men, indeed, suffer for Dishonesty, but for Poverty, many: The greatest Part of Mankind being Rogues within, or without the Law, so that little Thieves are hang'd for the Security of great ones. Take my Word, Sir, there are greater Rogues ride in their own Coaches, than any that walk on Foot; a poor Fellow shall be hang'd for Stealing to support Life, while many solemn Villains, with supercilious Faces and brush'd Beavers, that plunder whole Families, are complimented with the Title of Right Worshipful.[22]

A Woman's Revenge was slightly altered by an unknown hand and presented as an opera at the Haymarket Theatre in 1729 under the title of *Love and Revenge; or, The Vintner Outwitted*. Brainworm, Vizard's successor, is the same kind of philosophizing rogue and makes his anti-heroical observations many times in Vizard's own words.[23]

This anti-heroical spirit provides the chief link between low-life literature of the early eighteenth century and the rogue tradition which had long flourished on the Continent and in England. It proved useful to writers who wished to criticize or ridicule the chivalric idea: witness the *Roman de Renart*, the *Liber vagatorum*, the several accounts of Till Eulenspiegel, and certain of the fabliaux. For the present purpose the most relevant expression of this literary tradition is the picaresque tale,[24] which came into prominence as a separate type with the publication in 1554 of *La Vida de Lazarillo de Tormes*.

The picaresque tale presents the life-story of a *pícaro*, or lowborn vagabond. Frequently it takes the form of a mock-serious confessional; Guzmán de Alfarache, the central character of Mateo Alemán's most important work, is supposedly an old and reformed man rehearsing in a mood of repentance his life of roguish adventure. In the usual tale the *pícaro* spends his time, or a great part of it, in the employ of a series of masters, each one of whom he serves for the sole purpose, apparently, of robbing and cheating him. His period of service is never long, and, once discharged, he travels to the next city, seeks out another master, and continues his career of knavery. Knowing nothing of the distinction between *meum* and *tuum*, the *pícaro's* typical offense is theft, usually indirect. In the course of feeding his insatiable acquisitiveness, he resorts to all manner of tricks, jests, and cheats, which are intended to impose upon his victim. Being a humorist by nature and circumstance, the *picaro* takes delight in his devices and frequently uses them for no other purpose than to discomfit an innocent. He values ingenious trickery for its own sake, and the fact that his jests sometimes cause pain does not disturb him. Although an unmitigated rogue, the *picaro* is no villain. Such crimes as calculated murder, highway robbery, or housebreaking do not attract him. As F. W. Chandler says, he has "too much good nature and humor as well as too little resolution to wear the tragic mask. He may be as coarse and merciless as you will in his jests, but they are meant as jests to the last."[25]

Such a predisposition to knavery makes the rogue's life one long adventure, during the course of which he usually travels over the whole of Europe. His continual activity brings him into all sorts of violent and farcical situations. Usually his cleverness gives him the final advantage, but occasionally he falls victim to his own pranks. When this happens, he takes his beating stolidly and resolves to be sharper the next time.[26]

Social satire is an essential element in the picaresque tale. The rogue's actions, in which he takes great pride, are at the same time the petty and disreputable counterpart of the glorious deeds of his betters. The kinship between the hero and the anti-hero is real, whereas the disparity between their positions and fortunes is accidental. It is this paradox which, in F. W. Chandler's words, "is the core and center of every satirical romance of roguery, from the most insignificant Spanish *novelas* to Fielding's *Jonathan Wild the Great.*"[27] Social satire in the picaresque tale is expressed in words as well as implied in situation and action. Guzmán, for example, frequently discourses on the distinction which the world makes between great thieves and small. He says, on one occasion:

A thiefe, what will he not doe to steale, Which word Thiefe, I apply to such poore sinfull creatures as my selfe. As for your great rich theeves, such as . . . often hang such poor snakes as wee are, I have nothing to say to them. For we are farre inferiour unto them, and are those little fishes, which these great ones devoure.[28]

The merry jester Scapin disavows all intention of ever attempting "the great Rooks and Cheats allow'd by publick Authority," saying "that they ruin such little Undertraders as I am."[29]

The rogues of picaresque fiction regularly go beyond these invidious comparisons and praise their own deeds. Captain Rolando, chief of a gang of robbers, makes Gil Blas a long speech in defense of the proposition that there are no more honest folk in the world than thieves.[30] An old rascal in *The English Rogue* admonishes his protégé in these words:

My son . . . the profession of a thief is not of so base repute as the brave men have in former times exercised themselves in this way: I have heard the Clerk of our parish say . . . that *Robin Hood* that famous thief was in his younger dayes Earl of *Huntingdon;* and that *Alexander the Great* was no better than a thief in robbing other princes of their Kingdoms and Crowns.[31]

These three forms—eighteenth-century criminal biography, eighteenth-century low-life writing, and the picaresque tale—display remarkable resemblances. Conventions of the old rogue story appear in criminal biography. "Captain" Alexander Smith and his successor "Captain" Charles Johnson[32] with a fine freedom worked the familiar tricks and jests of picaresque fiction into their histories of genuine malefactors. The long narrative of low-life, particularly as written by Defoe, owes an obvious debt to the criminal biography.[33] The roguish gaiety of Macheath, the dashing hero of *The Beggar's Opera,* resembles the extravagant humor of many a *picaro.* Likewise, Peachum, although undoubtedly modeled on the actual Jonathan Wild, has spiritual kinsmen in picaresque literature and criminal biography. The *alguazil* of Spanish rogue fiction, a quasi-official bailiff and thief-catcher, is omnipresent and always hateful.[34] The infamy of the informer is the theme of Luke Hutton's *Blacke Dogge of Newgate* (c. 1600)[35] and of *The Life and Death of Griffin Flood* (1623); in *The English Rogue* thief-takers are frequently mentioned as evil creatures who must be strictly avoided. In short, these three forms are all manifestations of one of the most comprehensive of literary traditions—the tradition of realism.[36]

Fielding's *Jonathan Wild* contains some of the features of eighteenth-century criminal biography. Book I is an elaborate biographical account of Wild's life up to the time of his decision to place himself at the head of a gang. Jonathan comes of a roguish line, which, beginning with Wulfstan Wild, a contemporary of Hengist, includes some of the most illustrious cutpurses, turncoats, cheaters, and thieves of history.[37] The present Jonathan is the only son of Jonathan Wild the elder, a debtor's bailiff, and Elizabeth Hollow of Hockley-in-the-Hole. During this lady's pregnancy it became apparent that she was to bear a prodigy. She dreamed that she was enjoyed in the night by the gods Mercury and Priapus; further than that, she constantly desired to possess everything she saw and could not be satisfied unless she secured it by stealth. With a fine appropriateness Jonathan made his appearance in the world on the first day of the plague in 1665, but was not baptized until some years later when the Rev. Mr. Titus Oates administered the sacrament. At an early age Jonathan exhibited unmistakable signs of his genius; he improved himself at school and greatly profited by the instruction and example of Count La Ruse, a gamester temporarily lodged in Newgate. The Count introduced Jonathan into society, where he rapidly became a favorite. After a few exploits in which the young rogue displayed his greatness by securing virtually all the booty for himself, he determined to place himself in command of a gang and rob all mankind. Thus Jonathan Wild entered upon the career which made him great and famous.

The wholly fictitious but elaborate and straightforward detail of this sketch of Wild's early life resembles the common practice in the catchpenny rogue lives and probably represents Fielding's caricature of criminal biography as written by the denizens of Grub Street. The imitation is close and just enough exaggerated to be thoroughly ironic. A satirical attack on the criminal pamphlet might be expected of Fielding. Throughout his life he maintained the highest respect for serious and worthy biography, which he regarded as an excellent source of moral knowledge. Indeed, Fielding quarreled with history as it was conventionally written, because it emphasized mere events, dates, and places, and minimized men, whose characters to a great extent shaped the events.[38] Fielding's "histories," therefore, took the form of biographical narratives having a moral purpose. With such ideals Fielding undoubtedly found the ordinary criminal biography both artistically and morally objectionable. He had given humorous expression to his serious disapproval of Colley Cibber's *Apology* and Richardson's *Pamela,* two basically biographical works, in *An Apology for the Life of Mr. T—— C——,* in *Shamela,* and in *Joseph Andrews.* In a similar manner he expressed his dislike of criminal biography by presenting an exaggeration of its weaknesses.

Criminal biography is not the chief object of attack in *Jonathan Wild,* however, or even its provocation.[39] The rogue lives were uniformly short; to be a complete parody *Jonathan Wild* would have to resemble them in length as well as in tone. Furthermore, with the introduction of the Heartfrees in Book II the biographical structure of Book I is replaced by a dramatic structure which prevails through the rest of the work. The word "dramatic" is used advisedly here; Books II, III, and IV of *Jonathan Wild* contain a conflict which is absent from Book I. In a somewhat similar manner the first three books of *Tom Jones* follow an almost purely biographical pattern, whereas in the remaining fifteen the important happenings in the hero's life are worked into a more complicated dramatic scheme.[40] After Book I, then, *Jonathan Wild* ceases to be solely the biography of a great rogue.

In writing *Jonathan Wild* Fielding certainly had a more urgent moral and artistic purpose than the annihilation of eighteenth-century criminal biography. In a manner observable in many of his other works he fitted satire on the rogue life into *Jonathan Wild* and made that satire, without losing its integrity, serve his larger purpose. This dual use of otherwise incidental matter was one of Fielding's peculiar narrative skills, and it is nicely illustrated in his attack on criminal biography.

To the general low-life writings of the early eighteenth century Fielding was indebted for many details of setting and atmosphere.

A great part of the action of *Jonathan Wild* takes place either in Newgate itself or in the house of Mr. Geoffrey Snap, a bailiff charged with apprehending debtors. Mr. Snap's guests, his daughters Laetitia and Theodosia, several bailiffs, and assorted thieves and rogues live freely and more or less amicably under his roof. The only distinction between prisoners and free persons is made by a few barred doors, and even that distinction is not rigidly observed. This little society very much resembles that surrounding the Peachum household in *The Beggar's Opera*. The Newgate of *Jonathan Wild* is a perfectly conventional one. Prisoners, impounded often on the flimsiest evidence, find great difficulty in meeting the many fees and "garnishes" and even greater in securing release; certain bold and experienced inhabitants tyrannize over the others and do a profitable business in extortion; the prison presents a constant scene of riot and drunkenness, particularly on execution morning, which is the occasion for a general orgy.[41] Even if Fielding did acquaint himself with disreputable neighborhoods, as his detractors often charged, he had at his disposal a ready-made low-life setting. *Jonathan Wild* displays no convincing evidence of effort on Fielding's part to observe and record the facts anew; he used the conventional setting throughout the book.

Virtually a part of the setting and atmosphere of *Jonathan Wild* are the minor characters who surround Wild himself: Count La Ruse, Mr. Snap, Mr. Wild, Senior, Bagshot, Laetitia and Theodosia Snap, Molly Straddle, Thomas Fierce, Marybone, Fireblood, and the ordinary of Newgate. None of these characters, not even Laetitia Snap or Fireblood, has any real individuality.[42] These supernumeraries, who serve to make the reproduction of a roguish society complete, are conventional figures of low-life literature, representing the various shady occupations. Included in their number are a gamester, a bully, a footpad, a highwayman, a murderer, and several ladies of easy virtue. Such persons as these similarly form the background of *The Beggar's Opera, Moll Flanders, The Mohocks, The London Spy,* and other works which portray a disreputable society.[43]

Jonathan Wild resembles contemporary literature of low-life, finally, in containing satire on the manners and morals of fashionable society. In a sense the whole ironic portraiture of Wild as the great man reflects Fielding's contempt for men who achieve eminence solely because of their power, wealth, and position, irrespective of their virtue. More specifically, Fielding's attack on high-life is to be seen in his narration of the courtship and marriage of Laetitia Snap and Jonathan Wild. Laetitia and Jonathan are matched in the cradle itself; the alliance, their parents believe, will increase the power and dignity of both families. This predestination, however, does not mean that either has the least liking or respect for the other. Jonathan is impelled toward Laetitia only by lust, and she in turn is attracted only by his fortune and position. After a protracted period of wooing, during which neither of the lovers is at all restrained by that "mean, base, low Vice of Constancy," a settlement is reached and they are married. A dubious bliss prevails for a fortnight, after which the couple quarrel violently and fall into a state of mutual contempt and indifference as perfect as that existing between any fine lady and gentleman. Laetitia returns to her promiscuous amours, and Wild offers no protest, except to give violent expression to his outraged pride when the affair between his wife and his lieutenant Fireblood comes to his notice. Laetitia pays Jonathan a visit during his final imprisonment for the purpose of taunting him; they part forever as the best of enemies.

This history represents Fielding's *reductio ad absurdum* of the kind of high-life alliance which was based on nothing but interest. To Fielding such a marriage was no marriage at all. He attacked it vigorously in his social drama *The Modern Husband,* in his poem "To a Friend on the Choice of a Wife," and in numerous interpolated observations throughout his other works." Fielding's satire on high-life in *Jonathan Wild* parallels that in other specimens of low-life literature in its basic method. He transfers to low people the essentially vicious attitudes of their "betters," and thereby proves that fashionable folk escape reproach not because of their moral superiority but simply because of their social position. Low-life literature regularly stressed the falsity of judgment according to rank, and with this emphasis Fielding heartily sympathized.

At first sight *Jonathan Wild* seems to share a number of features with the picaresque tale. Censure of fashionable society, loveless marriages, active rogues, and greedy parasites are to be found in both. Fielding even mentions young Wild's great admiration for two of the famous *picaros* of literature—Scapin and Guzmán, the Spanish rogue.[45] But the similarity between *Jonathan Wild* and the picaresque tale is superficial rather than essential.[46] Satire on high-life is only a corollary of Fielding's larger moral proposition—that unrestrained selfishness, particularly when disguised, is responsible for most of the world's evil. The roguish adventures which form the action of *Jonathan Wild* do not take their place because of their simple narrative value, as do those in the picaresque tale, but because of their underlying ethical import. The amusing satire of the rogue story is an end in itself; the satire in *Jonathan Wild,* while frequently entertaining, contributes to the moral purpose.

Further than this, Jonathan Wild himself differs basically from the conventional picaresque hero. The *picaro,* being no more than a rogue, carefully avoids all the serious and violent crimes. Jonathan Wild is only part rogue; the other part of him is pure villain. No deed repels him. Murder, rape, and all kinds of treachery are for Wild simply the natural instruments for accomplishing his wishes. These methods differ radically from the cheats and jests on which the *picaro* relies; in all of *Jonathan Wild,* according to F. W. Chandler, "not a clever piece of roguery is borrowed from the classic collections, and nothing Wild does is notable as a device."[47] Moreover, Fielding ignored the all-important convention of the rogue's service under a series of masters. Wild holds a position of authority, not of servitude. He commands a gang of thieves who turn their booty over to him and accept whatever compensation he chooses to give. The *picaro* hopes by the use of his wits to maintain himself in a state just a little above that of mere subsistence. Jonathan Wild has no such limited desires; he aspires to possess all that he can see. Jonathan Wild's greatness is the quality which separates him from the hero of the picaresque tale.

Stating the relationship of *Jonathan Wild* to traditional rogue fiction is not a simple matter. An anti-heroical spirit invests both, and both are filled with specific declarations of that spirit. But the anti-heroism of *Jonathan Wild* far surpasses in intensity that of the picaresque tale. A wealth of realistic detail is to be found in both, but, for all its circumstantiality, *Jonathan Wild* has a quality of abstractness and unreality which markedly contrasts with the concreteness of the rogue story. In *Jonathan Wild,* as in most of his other works, Fielding was following in his individual fashion the critical, anti-romantic tradition, of which the picaresque tale and its related forms are a single expression. Consequently, *Jonathan Wild* is in certain respects parrallel to the rogue fiction of Spain, France, and England, but is not essentially derivative from it.

THE COMIC EPIC POEM IN PROSE

Obviously, an analysis of the bonds between *Jonathan Wild* and certain established literary types and traditions does not provide a full explanation of the form in which Fielding cast his work. The peculiarity of *Jonathan Wild* can be very simply stated: it represents an imperfect version of the comic epic poem in prose, a kind of writing which Fielding developed in his great novels.[48] It may be said by way of brief introduction that the ideas of the comic epic and the prose epic were not without precedent in practice and in critical theory.[49] The classic example of the comic poetic epic was *The Battle of the Frogs and Mice,* a heroic parody long ascribed to Homer and many times translated.[50] Some Renaissance critics, believing that imitation, not meter, constituted the essence of poetry, accepted prose as a possible medium of poetic expression. Accordingly, Julius Caesar Scaliger referred to Heliodorus's prose *Aethiopica* as a "model epic."[51] Le Bossu in the *Traité du poëme epique* (1675) and Madame Dacier, his disciple, fully justified the prose epic.[52] Fénélon attempted it in *Les Aventures de Télémaque* (1699), a work which was generally admired in the early eighteenth century and by none more than Fielding.

More pertinent is Fielding's own theory of the comic prose epic, which he discussed informally but carefully in the Preface to *Joseph*

Andrews. As conceived by Fielding, the comic prose epic is at once a form and a spirit. An examination of *Jonathan Wild* in the light of Fielding's theory will reveal those respects in which this work utilizes the form and embodies the spirit of the comic epic poem in prose.[53]

The formal essence of the comic prose epic, according to Fielding, consists in the adaptation of the technique of the serious epic to insignificant and undignified subject matter. The traditional elements of the serious epic are fable and action, characters, sentiments, and diction. The fable and the action which vivifies it must be grave and important; the characters must be persons of eminence, generally national heroes, and must possess "manners" which accord with their station; the sentiments must be lofty, and the language of the whole pure and elevated. The manner in which Fielding fitted these components of the serious epic into his comic scheme is simply stated in the Preface to *Joseph Andrews:*

It differs from the serious romance in its fable and action in this: that as in the one these are grave and solemn, so in the other they are light and ridiculous; it differs in its characters by introducing persons of inferior rank, and consequently of inferior manners, whereas the grave romance sets the highest before us; lastly, in its sentiments and diction, by preserving the ludicrous instead of the sublime. In the diction, I think, burlesque itself may sometimes be admitted. . . .

It will be noticed that in this statement Fielding is contrasting his comic theory with the theory of grave romance. Here, as in other passages, Fielding fails to observe a rigid distinction between the general terms "romance" and "epic," a failure for which there was ample critical precedent.[54] Indeed, in the same paragraph Fielding equates the comic epic poem in prose and the comic romance, the most notable examples of which are *Don Quixote* and *Le Roman comique* of Paul Scarron.[55] Both of these works contain some comic uses of epic devices.

Jonathan Wild does not fulfill all of the formal requirements for the comic epic poem in prose as set forth in the foregoing quotation. It would be hardly possible to regard the greatness-goodness conflict, which approximates a fable[56] or organizing theme,[57] as "light and ridiculous"; nor is the basic action—Wild's attempted annihilation of Heartfree and Heartfree's passive resistance—anything but grave. The characters of *Jonathan Wild,* however, fit well in a comic epic. Despite the constant ironical exaltation of Wild, the central character, he remains a low and unworthy person,[58] the very opposite of what the hero of a serious epic should be. Likewise, the disreputable crowd surrounding Wild, and even the Heartfrees, although morally irreproachable, occupy a social station far below that of the characters in a conventional epic. The "manners" of Wild and his crew are plainly both ignoble and vicious; those of the Heartfrees are, if not ignoble, at least "low" and unheroic. In the same way the "manners" not only of Mr. and Mrs. Tow-wouse and Parson Trulliber, but also of Parson Adams himself contrast violently with those of Aeneas and his noble Trojans. The characters of *Jonathan Wild,* then, fulfill the requirements of the comic prose epic.[59]

While the "sentiments"[60] in *Jonathan Wild* cannot be said to preserve exactly the "ludicrous instead of the sublime," they do represent perversions of the lofty pronouncements required of the serious epic. Such degradations of "sentiments" are to be found chiefly in comments on Wild's character and actions, in Wild's speeches, and in general ironic moral observations. For example, one of the fifteen maxims which Jonathan Wild left for the edification of his successors proposes: "That many Men were undone by not going deep enough in Roguery, as in Gaming any Man may be a Loser who doth not play the whole Game."[61] During his ascent to greatness he suffers a temporary discomfiture when Count La Ruse absconds with the jewels stolen from Heartfree and leaves Wild in possession of some cheap imitations. The great man, having lamented his ill fortune, consoles himself thus:

Why then should any Man wish to be a Prig, or where is his GREATNESS? I answer, in his Mind: 'Tis the inward Glory, the secret Consciousness of doing great and wonderful Actions, which can alone support the truly GREAT Man, whether he be a CONQUEROR, a TYRANT, a MINISTER, or a PRIG.

These must bear him up against the private Curse and public Imprecation, and while he is hated and detested by all Mankind, must make him inwardly satisfied with himself.[62]

In another passage Fielding ironically gives as a general lesson to be drawn from Wild's conduct the following advice: *"Tho' as a Christian thou art obliged, and we advise thee to forgive thy Enemy,* NEVER TRUST THE MAN WHO HATH REASON TO SUSPECT THAT YOU KNOW HE HATH INJURED YOU."[63] Many more such passages could be cited. Fielding found the inverted "sentiment" peculiarly effective as a vehicle for ethical satire, and he used it without stint.

The use of ludicrous, and even burlesque,[64] diction in *Jonathan Wild* is most apparent in certain elaborate mock-epic similes and in heroic epithets. The confinement of the Count and Bagshot, for example, is made the subject of this extravagant epic comparison:

As when their Lap is finished, the cautious Huntsman to their Kennels gathers the nimble-footed Hounds, they with lank Ears and Tails slouch sullenly on, whilst he with his Whippers-in follows close at their Heels, regardless of their dogged Humour, till having seen them safe within the Door, he turns the Key, and then retires to whatever Business or Pleasure calls him thence: So with louring Countenance, and reluctant steps mounted the Count and *Bagshot* to their Chamber, or rather Kennel, whither they were attended by *Snap,* and those who followed him, and where *Snap* having seen them deposited, very contentedly locked the Door, and departed.[65]

The phrase "nimble-footed Hounds" in the foregoing passage provides a good illustration of burlesque epithet. Others are more common. Jonathan is, of course, regularly "the great," and Laetitia Snap is at first "the chaste" and then "the fair."[66] Most of the ludicrous diction in *Jonathan Wild* is not distinctive enough to merit quotation. Fielding regularly, almost habitually, narrates vulgar or unseemly actions and describes drab, ugly, or grotesque scenes in high-flown language. The incongruity between subject and expression aids in providing "the surprising absurdity" which is characteristic of the comic epic.

The comic epic imitates its serious counterpart in certain specific conventions as well as in general matters of style. Fielding does not mention the digression, the discovery, or the marvelous in his prefatory theory; such epic devices, however, are to be found not only in *Joseph Andrews,* an avowed comic prose epic, but also in *Jonathan Wild.*

The "digression," usually in the form of an interpolated story, was a favorite device of Fielding and of writers of fiction before him. *Don Quixote* and *Le Roman comique,* the two notable comic romances, are filled with incidental stories. The most famous in Cervantes' masterpiece are the "novel" of the Curious Impertinent, and the story of the shepherdess Marcella. *Le Roman comique* contains well over half a dozen interpolated tales, some of them past histories of main characters and some unrelated "novels."[67] *Joseph Andrews* is interrupted by the histories of Leonora and of Mr. Wilson. The chief digressive tale in *Jonathan Wild* is contained in the five chapters which relate Mrs. Heartfree's adventures after her escape from the lustful Wild.[68] Transferring from ship to ship she wanders over a large area of the South Atlantic and through a goodly portion of the continent of Africa in her attempts to return to England and her husband. In the course of these wanderings she not only endures shipwreck, hunger, thirst, and fatigue, but also resists, in a manner distinctly reminiscent of Pamela, no less than a dozen attempts on her chastity. To climax these amazing adventures, she encounters Count La Ruse and recovers the jewels with which he had absconded.

In addition to being an unmistakable interpolated narrative, these chapters are an obvious satire on the fantastic travel tale. In one day's march, for example, the shipwrecked company encounters a monster shaped like Windsor Castle, a quarter-mile-long snake, the celebrated phoenix-bird, and a bed of pumpkins each one as large as Stonehenge.[69] Mrs. Heartfree's indefatigable defense of her virtue was probably intended as a ridiculous imitation of Pamela's steadfast resistance.[70] This interpolated tale—an epic device comically used—again illustrates Fielding's ability to accomplish several purposes at once.[71]

"Discovery," which might be defined as the revelation at a crucial moment of a fact which changes the course of action and brings the narrative to a culmination, was a regular feature of the epic, serious and comic alike.[72] In *Joseph Andrews* the formula of discovery is employed in the disclosure of the fact that Joseph is not Fanny's brother but actually the long lost son of Mr. Wilson. This revelation effects a reversal. The barrier to marriage raised by the lovers' supposed kinship is removed and the way is cleared for a rapid conclusion. In *Jonathan Wild* discovery plays its part when the bearer of Heartfree's last-minute reprieve brings the news that Fireblood's confession has cleared the jeweler and virtually condemned Wild. By this single event the situation is reversed; Wild goes on to the consummation of his greatness and Heartfree to the reättainment of his modest felicity.

Somewhat allied to the formula of "discovery" is the convention of the "marvelous." The use of this device is a familiar feature of the ancient epic, in which gods and goddesses, or their agents, frequently intervene in the conflicts of the characters to influence and alter the action. The proper disposition of the marvelous always presented serious problems of probability and verisimilitude, even after the pagan epic had been displaced by the so-called Christian epic. In evolving a theory of the comic epic Fielding naturally encountered the problem of the marvelous and, partly because of the unheroic nature of comic material, easily solved it. In a chapter of *Tom Jones* devoted to a discourse on the marvelous, having expressed the wish "that Homer could have known the rule prescribed by Horace, to introduce supernatural agents as seldom as possible,"[73] Fielding excludes elves, fairies, "and other such mummery" from the modern marvelous and admits only ghosts, used sparingly. He concludes the marvelous in comic epic is simply the surprising and that the modern writer may use it effectively only by staying within the boundaries of credibility.

With a considerable show of pseudo learning, Fielding injects this theory, incompletely formulated, into *Jonathan Wild*. After Wild's frustrated attempt on Mrs. Heartfree's virtue, the chivalrous sea captain casts him adrift in a small boat. Wild convinces himself that he prefers drowning to a slow death from starvation and thirst, and accordingly plunges into the sea. Within two minutes he is "miraculously . . . replaced in his Boat; and this without the assistance of a Dolphin or Sea-Horse, or any other Fish or Animal, who are always . . . ready at Hand when a Poet or Historian pleases to call for them to carry a Hero through a Sea."[74] Digressing briefly, Fielding tells his readers with mock solemnity that he chooses to obey the rule of Horace, *"Nec Deus intersit nisi dignus vindice nodus."* Nature is a sufficient guide for a poet concerned with human beings. This "Great *Alma Mater* Nature," he continues, has ordained the gallows as the proper finishing-place of Jonathan Wild's career. Intent, then, on seeing her decrees fulfilled, she simply whispers in his ear that immediate death by drowning has immediate discomforts and urges him to return to the boat. Obedient to his fate, he forthwith does so. Thus an event which at first seemed explicable only in terms of the "marvelous" is actually no more than surprising. With considerable use of critical jargon, Fielding turns to comic use another device of the serious epic.

Just as the formal characteristics of the comic prose epic imitate those of the serious epic, so the spirit of Fielding's new kind of writing presents a counterpart of the traditional epic temper. The serious epic concerns the sublime in human nature; the comic prose epic treats the ridiculous. In the Preface to *Joseph Andrews* Fielding carefully states his theory of the ridiculous. This quality has its true source in affectation, which in turn derives from either of two causes—vanity or hypocrisy. Hypocrisy, because it represents direct opposition to truth, generates a more striking affectation than does vanity; "our Ben Jonson," says Fielding, "who of all men understood the Ridiculous the best, hath chiefly used the hypocritical affectation." The revelation of affectation produces the ridiculous in writing and both surprises and pleases the reader who admires the natural and scorns the false.

Ridicule, however, must be used with care and discrimination. The "misfortunes and calamities of life, or the imperfections of nature" do not in themselves present objects for ridicule. The humpbacked man, for example, becomes a proper victim only if he affects strength or handsomeness. Neither do great crimes and vices come within the province of the ridiculous; these can be regarded only with abhorrence, not with amusement. Fielding takes care, furthermore, to distinguish the ridiculous from a spirit which superficially resembles it, the burlesque. The burlesque in writing, like the "caricatura" in painting, represents the monstrous and unnatural, whereas the true ridiculous never departs from nature.[75] To call "the ingenious Hogarth" a burlesque painter, says Fielding, would be both inaccurate and dishonorable, for Hogarth never really violates or falsifies nature. The burlesque has, to be sure, a valuable place in the diction of the comic prose epic, but none in the conception.

Thus the comic prose epic takes on a corrective and didactic aspect. By exposing affectation, in either or both of its forms, the writer of the comic epic helps his readers to look through appearance and see reality. The amusement which attends this process fortifies its value. In brief, the comic prose epic, as conceived by Fielding, is an admirable medium for conveying both delight and instruction.

Fielding's theory of the ridiculous is not entirely original. A number of his predecessors and contemporaries saw the basis of comedy in affectation. Shaftesbury, whom Fielding mentions in his Preface, made ridicule a test of truth. In *Sensus communis* he advocates ridicule "a lenitive remedy against vice, and a kind of specific against superstition and melancholy delusion."[76] Fielding also mentions the Abbé Bellegarde as a theorist of the ridiculous. Bellegarde did indeed devote the two volumes of his *Reflexions sur ridicule* to the subject. Like Fielding, he made the connection between affectation and the ridiculous: "Affectation is *the falsification of the whole Person, which deviates from all that is Natural, whereby it might please, to put on an ascititious Ayre, wherewithal to become Ridiculous.*"[77] The Abbé Bellegarde, according to Fielding's view, "shows us many species of it" [the ridiculous] but does not once "trace it to its fountain." Citing La Rochefoucauld as his authority, a writer in

Common Sense, a journal with which Fielding was associated, takes as the text for an extensive essay the notion that "People are never ridiculous from their real, but from their affected Characters."[78]

Fielding's idea of the ridiculous fits nicely into the theory of the comic prevalent in the early eighteenth century. "Incongruity of style or character" was the general basis of corrective comedy;[79] Fielding in his theory of the comic prose epic simply stressed one kind of incongruity, that which originates in affectation.

In *Jonathan Wild* the ridiculous appears in the character of Wild himself. Vanity plays an incidental part in his personality, but hypocrisy is almost his fundamental trait.[80] In his final summary of Wild Fielding says:

The Character which he most valued himself upon, and which he principally honored in others, was that of Hypocrisy. His Opinion was that no one could carry *Priggism* very far without it; for which Reason, he said, there was little GREATNESS to be expected in a Man who acknowledged his Vices. . . .[81]

Examples of the operation of Wild's hypocrisy are numerous. It is his first device for imposing upon the members of his gang; only when forced does he resort to bullying. His professions and apparently generous actions long deceive the unsuspicious but not unintelligent Heartfree. Only after the most flagrant evidence of duplicity does the victimized jeweler reluctantly become disillusioned. So persuasive is Wild's oratory that the prisoners of Newgate, a group presumably not characterized by gullibility, eagerly set him up as their dictator.

Like Wild Fireblood, a "second-rate GREAT MAN," is noted for hypocrisy. Although the two are in constant association, Wild does not until near the end suspect that his faithful lieutenant has been carrying on an affair with Laetitia, and apparently the great man never discovers that Fireblood lodged the information which led to the final arrest and condemnation. Laetitia, on the other hand, is actuated chiefly by vanity. It is her persistent desire to play the lady of fashion. To that end she assumes airs, encourages gallants, and despises her husband. Like a great lady she enjoys her own vices, but affects to be greatly shocked by others'. When her sister Theodosia bears Count La Ruse's child, Laetitia damns her for besmirching the family honor and refuses ever to see her again.

Fielding places Jonathan, Fireblood, and Laetitia in the category of the ridiculous simply by exposing their actions. It was not necessary for Fielding to belabor his victims; the difference between their professions and their practices, between the appearance and the reality of their characters, is patent. Indeed, throughout his Preface to *Joseph Andrews* Fielding never once mentions the scourging of affectation. Such treatment is proper only for great vices; for the ridiculous simple exposure is quite enough.

The spirit of the comic prose epic is, with certain modifications, quite consistent with the ethical import of *Jonathan Wild*. It is only proper that the unmasking of hypocritical affectation should have an important part in the history of greatness. Indeed, exposure of vice is Fielding's aim. In the Preface to the *Miscellanies,* he concludes his own comments on *Jonathan Wild* with this statement: "This Greatness then is the Character I intend to expose; and the more this prevails in and deceives the World, taking to itself not only Riches and Power, but often Honour, or at least the Shadow of it, the more necessary it is to strip the Monster of these false Colours, and shew it in its native Deformity...."[82] The very essence of greatness is hypocrisy; the powerful politician, the tyrant, the conqueror, differ from the prig only in position and reputation. Fielding was, during his entire literary career, intent on penetrating false appearances. In *Jonathan Wild* satire on fashionable society, the attack on greatness, and the exposure of the affectation which springs from hypocrisy are simply different expressions of Fielding's abiding moral purpose.

The foregoing discussion suggests one of the respects in which *Jonathan Wild* fails to agree with the spirit of the comic prose epic as Fielding's describes it in the Preface to *Joseph Andrews*. Wild's hypocrisy brings him into the realm of the ridiculous, but his villainy is beyond it. In his persecution of Heartfree Wild employs robbery and treachery and intends murder. "Great vices," says Fielding in outlining his theory, "are the proper objects of . . . detestation," not of amusement. It has already been pointed out that Wild is sometimes a rogue and sometimes a villain.[83] Therefore, he is subject now to ridicule, now to hatred.

Furthermore, Fielding carefully excludes the burlesque from the comic prose epic with the single exception of its place in diction. The burlesque represents the monstrous and unnatural, whereas the true ridiculous adheres closely to nature. In *Jonathan Wild,* however, burlesque enters into both the characterization and the action. Fireblood first appears as a monstrous and unnatural character. He has in his makeup "not one Grain" of humanity, modesty, or fear. He welcomes Wild's proposal to commit murder with a remark to the effect that *"D——n his Eyes, he thought there was no better Pastime than blowing a Man's Brains out."*[84] Fireblood's actions bear out this characterization with an undeviating consistency. Likewise, Wild and Laetitia are in certain respects burlesque characters. She is excessively ugly in body, mind, and deed. The "dialogue matrimonial" which passes between Wild and Laetitia a fortnight after their marriage is a gross exaggeration of marital strife, as is their final violent parting in Newgate. In virtually every scene between Wild and Laetitia comedy gives way to burlesque.

The comic prose epic, finally, makes no allowance for other than incidental irony. One of the most spectacular features of *Jonathan Wild* is the ironical adulation which Fielding heaps upon his central character. Greatness, the quality which brings mischief on mankind, is presented as the sublime in human nature. Wild proceeds from triumph to triumph until he attains the final exaltation of the great man—hanging. By ironical contrast the traits of character which dominate Heartfree are low, mean, and pitiable. Fielding maintains this artificial attitude quite consistently; occasionally— perhaps to relieve his readers, perhaps more vigorously to express his own moral wrath—he reverses his usual attitude and for a brief time roundly condemns greatness. But he always returns to the basic paradox. The irony which dominates *Jonathan Wild* is utterly serious in intent. Fielding is concerned with exposing evil, not faults and failings. *Joseph Andrews* and *Tom Jones* are fundamentally good-humored works, in which serious vices "are rather the accidental consequences of some human frailty or foible, than causes habitually existing in the mind." In *Jonathan Wild* the situation is reversed. The sustained irony reveals an evil which is fundamental; it is the humorous unmasking of affectation which occasionally seems incidental.

To the extent that *Jonathan Wild* is not representative of the spirit of the comic prose epic, it is not a close imitation of nature. It is rather a moral allegory, in which the two central characters are not so much men as opposing symbols. The action is determined and directed by the moral end and the work as a whole is likely to leave an impression of purposeful artificiality.

Jonathan Wild, then, is an imperfect comic epic poem in prose. Both in form and in spirit it fulfills to a limited degree the requirements as set forth by Fielding himself. If it could be established that Fielding conceived and at least partially wrote *Jonathan Wild* before *Joseph Andrews,* one could go a step further and say that *Jonathan Wild* is a narrative forecast of the form which Fielding employed in his great novels.

SYNTHESIS

This study, now to be concluded, has been concerned with the facts and traditions available to Fielding and the form in which they are cast. The prototype of Fielding's Jonathan Wild became notorious in London between 1718 and 1725, acquired an evil reputation, and finally died on the gallows amid great public applause. The ephemeral writings inspired by his death added, either satirically or straightforwardly, to his monstrous reputation, and thereby influenced the popular mind to regard Wild more as a symbol of evil than as an individual. This process of symbolization was continued in the propaganda of the Opposition to Walpole. Because of the connotation of his name, the Opposition writers found the satirical coupling of Jonathan Wild and the Prime Minister an effective political device. The thief and the statesman were paralleled, frequently to the latter's disadvantage, many times between 1725 and 1742, the year of Walpole's fall. In this manner the name Jonathan Wild and its symbolic significance remained current, while his actual history and individuality virtually disappeared. In writing *Jonathan Wild* Henry Fielding utilized some genuine biographical material. Far more important, however, is his adoption and extended use of the symbolized character. The Jonathan Wild of Fielding's life is to a great extent the Jonathan Wild of the Opposition writers. Since Fielding was sympathetic with the ideals if not the policies of the Opposition, he made the usual attack on Walpole. The political satire in *Jonathan Wild,* however, has an ethical, not a partisan basis. Jonathan Wild stands for something more fundamental and universal than an arbitrary and corrupt statesman. He is a personification not merely of political but of general evil.

Thus symbolized, Jonathan Wild takes his place in the ethical conflict which provides the motivation of the whole work—the conflict between greatness and goodness. Greatness, a term which signifies inordinate personal ambition, was a common theme among popular moralists of Fielding's time. These writers insisted that the great man, whether statesman, tyrant, conqueror, or exalted rogue, was the constant enemy of mankind. Opposed to the great man in popular ethics stood the good man, in whose character predatoriness was replaced by a fundamental beneficence. This contrast between greatness and goodness represented a simplified version of formal and learned ethical speculation, which centered on the presence and operation in man of self-love and benevolence.

Fielding was greatly interested in the conflict between greatness and goodness. In many of his poems, essays, and dramas written before *Jonathan Wild* he took occasion implicitly or explicitly to condemn greatness and applaud goodness. *Jonathan Wild* represents his most extended use of this simple moral opposition. Jonathan Wild personifies greatness, Thomas Heartfree goodness, and both exhibit the extreme simplification characteristic of personified abstractions. Wild conducts a thoroughgoing campaign to rob, disgrace, and murder Heartfree, whose resistance is almost wholly passive. In the end Wild goes to the gallows, and Heartfree returns to a life of peace and prosperity. The whole action centers on the unsuccessful attack of greatness on unassertive but unconquerable goodness. *Jonathan Wild* may be called, therefore, an allegorical presentation of a fundamental moral theme.

It is impossible to label the form into which the biographical, political, and ethical substance of *Jonathan Wild* is cast. Although it follows a prose narrative pattern, it is plainly not a novel. It contains elements of the sensationalized criminal biography popular in the early part of the eighteenth century. Likewise it shares certain characteristics with other low-life writings of that period and with the classic picaresque tale. A somewhat better explanation of the form of *Jonathan Wild* follows from the comparison of this work with Fielding's conception of the comic epic poem in prose. In most matters of technique and spirit *Jonathan Wild* nicely satisfies Fielding's requirements for the comic prose epic; in certain respects, however, it fails to fulfill them.

It is likely that Fielding, being far less concerned with form than with substance, was content, perhaps unconsciously, to mix without fusing elements from previously existing literary modes and from his own form, the comic prose epic. In general, *Jonathan Wild* incorporates these elements into a biographical narrative pattern, a form which because of its very looseness is best adapted to a digressive, moralizing, allegorical tale.

As a study in the selection and adaptation of factual and traditional materials and in the shaping of these materials according to a governing moral purpose, Fielding's *Jonathan Wild* presents an interesting problem in literary form and technique. As a date in the history of ideas, this work demonstrates the effect upon one of the great writers of the eighteenth century of contemporary political and ethical thought. In itself, *Jonathan Wild* is important as a product of the genius which was to portray an age in the microcosm of *Tom Jones*. *Jonathan Wild the Great* is Henry Fielding writ small, but Henry Fielding still.

NOTES

Notes

I. BIOGRAPHICAL AND HISTORICAL BACKGROUND

[1] See [Anonymous], *Weighley, alias Wild* (1725), pp. 30–31, and Daniel Defoe, *A True and Genuine Account of the Life and Actions of Jonathan Wild . . .* in *Romances and Narratives of Daniel Defoe*, ed. by George Aitken (1895), XVI, 235–78. In 1692 the government had begun paying blood money for the apprehension of criminals. See Frank W. Chandler, *The Literature of Roguery* (1907), I, 158.

[2] *An Answer to a Late Insolent Libel . . .* [1718], reprinted in F. J. Lyons, *Jonathan Wild, Prince of Robbers* [1936], p. 253. There is no way of identifying the hack writer who composed this defense of Wild.

[3] *The British Journal*, CXXXVI (April 24, 1725).

[4] [Anonymous], *An Authentick Narrative of the Life and Actions of Jonathan Wild . . .* (1725), p. 7.

[5] *The Political State of Great Britain*, XXIX (May, 1725), 506.

[6] *Common Sense; or, The Englishman's Journal*, December 23, 1738.

[7] *The British Journal*, CXXVIII (February 27, 1724/25).

[8] *Ibid.*, CXXIX (March 6, 1725).

[9] Daniel Defoe, *The Life and Actions of Jonathan Wild*, p. 250.

[10] The "superannuated Thief" was, according to most accounts, the accomplished pirate Roger Johnson, who is used as a character in Book IV of Fielding's *Jonathan Wild*. See *A Full and Particular Account of the Life and Notorious Transactions of Roger Johnson . . .* (1740), pp. 16–17, 18–19.

[11] *The Political State of Great Britain*, XXIX, 505–6.

[12] *The Complete Newgate Calendar . . .* (1926), III, 25.

[13] Daniel Defoe, *op. cit.*, p. 262.

[14] Apparently Jonathan Wild's name was automatically associated with the London underworld. *The Universal Journal*, an imitator of *The Tatler*, during all of 1723 and 1724 labeled its paragraphs of criminal intelligence "from Jonathan Wilde's in the Old-Bailey." See particularly Nos. 13, 19, 21, 25, 26, 32, 35, 37.

[15] *The Whitehall Evening Post*, No. 525 (January 20, 1722).

[16] *The British Journal*, LXVIII (January 4, 1723/24). See also LXXXIII (April 18, 1724); LXXXVIII (May 23, 1724); *Applebee's Journal*, June 6, 1724, as reprinted in William Lee, *Daniel Defoe; His Life and Recently Discovered Writings* (1869), III, 271; and *The Daily Post*, November 2, 1724.

[17] *Weighley, alias Wild*, p. 10.

[18] Daniel Defoe, *The Lives of Six Notorious Street Robbers*, in *Romances and Narratives . . .* XVI, 357–60.

[19] Wild had been pursuing Blueskin for almost two years; he was one of a number of suspected highwaymen captured by Wild in 1722. See *The British Journal*, XV (December 29, 1722).

[20] Daniel Defoe, *The History of the Remarkable Life of John Sheppard*, in *Romances and Narratives . . .* XVI, 198.

[21] He was hanged on November 12, 1724. See *Parker's London News . . .*, No. 935 (November 13, 1724).

[22] CIX (October 17, 1724).

[23] Daniel Defoe, *Lives of Six Notorious Street Robbers*, p. 360.

[24] *Applebee's Journal*, August 1, 1724, reprinted in W. Lee, *Daniel Defoe* . . . III, 288.

[25] *Applebee's Journal*, November 7, 1724, *ibid.*, III, 330.

[26] See *The British Journal*, CXV. Accompanying the account of Thornhill's visit is a set of complimentary verses. The first and last stanzas read:

> "Thornhill, 'tis thine to gild with Fame
> The obscure, and raise the humble Name;
> To make the Form elude the Grave,
> And *Sheppard* from oblivion save.
>
> .   .   .
>
> *Apelles Alexander* drew,
> *Caesar* is to *Aurelius* due;
> *Cromwell* in *Lely's* Work doth shine,
> And *Sheppard, Thornhill*, lives in thine."

[27] See *The Prison-Breaker; or, The Adventures of John Sheppard* . . . (1725), 1.

[28] A. Knapp and W. Baldwin, *The New Newgate Calendar* . . . [n.d.], I, 267.

[29] *The Remarkable Life of John Sheppard*, p. 191.

[30] It is certain that for some time Wild's gang had been growing more and more rebellious, and would have been happy to have "impeached" him. See *Weighley, alias Wild*, pp. 17–18.

[31] Daniel Defoe, *The Life and Actions of Jonathan Wild*, p. 270.

[32] *The Life and Notorious Transactions of Roger Johnson* . . . pp. 18–19.

[33] A. Knapp and W. Baldwin, *The New Newgate Calendar* . . . I, 328. See above, p. 6. It is likely that this law had been revived and slightly changed for use against Wild. Defoe refers to it as "the new Act . . . which makes it a Felony . . . to Receive and Return Stolen Goods, Knowing them to be so and not apprehending and prosecuting the Felon. . . ." (*Applebee's Journal*, May 22, 1725, in W. Lee, *Daniel Defoe* . . . III, 386.) The pertinent part of this law is reproduced in black letter in the introduction to Bernard Mandeville's *Enquiry into the Causes of the Frequent Executions at Tyburn* . . . (1725), [Sig. A₈].

[34] See *The British Journal*, CXXIX (March 6, 1725).

[35] *Ibid.*, CXXIV (April 10, 1725).

[36] Two members of Wild's gang, Thomas Butler and John Fullwood, received pardons for being material witness against him. (*The British Journal*, CXXV, April 17, 1725.)

[37] One report states: "He endeavour'd to convince People, that at *Wolverhampton* he knew several Persons that would have proved his Friends, had he thought his Case dangerous, and timely applied to them. . . ." (*The Political State of Great Britain*, XXIX, 507.)

[38] See F. J. Lyons, *op. cit.*, pp. 298–302.

[39] "The Chronological Diary for the Year 1725," in *The Historical Register* . . . p. 21.

[40] See *Mist's Weekly Journal*, No. 4 (May 22, 1725).

[41] *The Political State of Great Britain*, XXIX, 509.

[42] *Ibid.*, p. 510.

[43] John Byrom, *Miscellaneous Poems* (1773), I, 20–21.

[44] *Applebee's Journal*, May 29, 1725, in W. Lee, *Daniel Defoe* . . . III, 389.

[45] Page 5. Hitchin's name does not appear on the title page of this pamphlet; it was supposedly written "by a Prisoner in Newgate."

[46] Ibid., p. 22.

[47] Ibid., p. 9.

[48] Ibid., p. 4.

[49] Ibid., p. 16.

[50] This woodcut is obviously an adaptation of an earlier woodcut of a hanging, in the Pepysian Collection. This earlier version is reproduced in Frank Aydelotte, *Elizabethan Rogues and Vagabonds* (1913), p. 71.

[51] Reprinted in F. J. Lyons, op. cit., pp. 248–83. Lyons also reproduces the title page; it bears the name "JONATHAN WILD, T. T.—'Thief-Taker'."

[52] Ibid., pp. 252–53.

[53] Hitchin's attack may have reached a fairly wide audience. Lyons states that he issued "pamphlet after pamphlet," in the hope of damaging Wild's business. (*Ibid.*, p. 224.)

[54] See *A Collection of Miscellany Letters, Selected out of Mist's Weekly Journal* (1722), I, 147. The letter referred to, No. XLIX, is undated. Letter No. L is dated November 14, 1719.

[55] *The Thieves Grammar* [c. 1720], p. 349.

[56] Ibid., p. 343.

[57] *A Narrative of all the Robberies, Escapes, &c. of John Sheppard*, in *Romances and Narratives* ... XVI, 222.

[58] *The Poems of Jonathan Swift*, ed. by Harold Williams (1937), III, 1113. (By permission of The Clarendon Press, Oxford.) Williams notes that "Blueskin's Ballad," sometimes attributed to John Gay, appeared immediately after the event in several broadside editions and achieved considerable popularity. It was sung during an interlude in John Thurmond's *Harlequin Sheppard* ... (1724).

Swift used Wild's name a second time. In the ballad "Clever Tom Clinch going to be Hanged" Tom says:

"My honest Friend *Wild*, may he long hold his Place,
He lengthen'd my Life with a whole Year of Grace."
(*Ibid.*, II, 399.)

[59] Sheppard was executed on November 16, 1724. See J. Thurmond, op. cit., p. 7.

[60] F. W. Chandler states that Defoe wrote this life of Sheppard before his death, and then pretended to receive the manuscript from Sheppard's hands on the morning of the execution. This biography ran through seven editions in a month. (*The Literature of Roguery*, I, 162.) It is interesting to note the similarity between Defoe's use of the autobiographical pose in this biography and in his longer narratives of low-life.

[61] *Romances and Narratives* ... XVI, 222. The confused style noticeable in this passage is typical of the whole.

[62] Allardyce Nicoll, *A History of Early Eighteenth Century Drama, 1700–1750* (1929), p. 244. Mark Longaker calls it "one of the most popular stage spectacles of the season," but gives no authority for his statement. (See *English Biography in the Eighteenth Century* [1931], p. 131.) S. M. Ellis states that Colley Cibber had a hand in *Harlequin Sheppard*. (Horace Bleackley and S. M. Ellis, *Jack Sheppard* ... [1933], p. 71.)

[63] J. Thurmond, op. cit., p. 15.

[64] W. E. Schultz believes that the printed copy of this play may have been a source for *The Beggar's Opera*. (*Gay's Beggar's Opera; Its Content, History, and Influence* [1923], p. 170.) Nicoll records no performance of *The Prison-Breaker*.

[65] *The Prison-Breaker*, Act I, scene 1, p. 4.

[66] *Ibid.*, Act II, scene 2, p. 47.

[67] CXVIII and CXXIX (February 27, 1724/25 and March 6, 1724/25). These articles were reprinted a few months later as the first two chapters in Mandeville's *Enquiry into the Causes of the Frequent Executions at Tyburn*. . . . Page references are to this work.

[68] The *N. E. D.* defines "theftbote" thus: "The taking of some payment from a thief to secure him from legal prosecution; either the receiving back by the owner of the stolen goods, or of some compensation, or the taking of a bribe by a person who ought to have brought the thief to justice." (IX, Part 2, 266.)

[69] *Enquiry* . . . p. 2.

[70] *Ibid.*, p. 8.

[71] *Ibid.*, pp. 15–16.

[72] Daniel Defoe, *The Life and Actions of Jonathan Wild*, p. 239.

[73] No. 5 (May 29, 1725).

[74] Reprinted in H. Bleackley and S. M. Ellis, *Jack Sheppard* . . . p. 204.

[75] *Ibid.*, p. 203.

[76] *Ibid.*, pp. 239–40.

[77] Published July 31, 1725. (*Mist's Weekly Journal*, No. 14.)

[78] *Weighley, alias Wild*, p. 4.

[79] See above, p. 16.

[80] Page 41.

[81] *Ibid.*, p. 6.

[82] The following is a list of other contemporary biographies, all of which are at present unavailable:

1. [Anonymous], *An Authentic History of the Parentage . . . Education . . . and Practices of J . . . W . . .* Stamford [1725?]. [British Museum.]

2. —— *The History of the Lives and Actions of J. W. . . . J. Blake, alias Blueskin . . . and J. Sheppard . . . Taken from Several Papers Found since Jonathan's Death . . .* London [1725]. [British Museum.]

3. —— *The Life of Jonathan Wilde, Thief-Taker-General of Great Britain and Ireland . . .* Northampton (1725). [See Aurélien Digeon, *Les Romans de Fielding* (1923), pp. 124–25.]

4. —— *The Life and Actions of . . . J. Wilde*, Gloucester [1725]. [British Museum.]

5. —— *The Life and Glorious Actions of the most Heroick and Magnanimous Jonathan Wild . . .* London [1725]. [See *Monthly Catalogue . . .* II (May, 1725), 56.]

6. —— *The Whole Proceedings of the Tryal of J. W., who was Try'd and Condemn'd at . . . the Old-Bailey, the 15th of May, 1725*, London [1725]. [British Museum.]

7. Puyney [Purney], Thomas, *The Ordinary of Newgate his Account of the Behaviour, last Dying Speeches and Confessions of the four Malefactors who were Executed at Tyburn . . . the 24th of May, 1725*, London [1725]. [British Museum.]

8. Smith, Capt. Alexander, *Memoirs of the Life and Times of the famous Jonathan Wild; together with the History and Lives of modern Rogues . . . Never before made Publick*, London [1726]. [See *Monthly Catalogue . . .* II (July, 1726), 76.]

[83] *Miscellanies by Henry Fielding, Esq.* (1743), I, xvi. [Preface.]

[84] Paul Dottin, *Daniel Defoe et ses romans* (1924), p. 257. It is difficult to decide whether this multiplication of editions is to be taken as evidence of great popularity, or as the sign of a publisher's trick. Another piece, *The Life of Jonathan Wild, by*

H. D. late Clerk to Justice R[aymond], was once thought to be Defoe's. G. A. Aitken, however, rejects it.

[85] Page 236.

[86] *Ibid.*, pp. 238–39.

[87] *Ibid.*, p. 263.

[88] *Ibid.*, p. 272.

[89] This is undoubtedly the tone of *The Life and Glorious Actions of the most Heroick and Magnanimous Jonathan Wild.* . . . Aurélien Digeon finds the same spirit in *The Life of Jonathan Wild, Thief-Taker-General of Great Britain and Ireland.* Digeon goes on to observe: "Jonathan Wild, ayant compté parmi les plus redoutables [des brigands], compta donc parmi les plus moqués." (*Les Romans de Fielding,* p. 126.)

[90] *The History of Henry Fielding* (1918), I, 408.

[91] *Ibid.*

[92] *The Literary Opposition to Sir Robert Walpole, 1721–1742,* University of Chicago dissertation (1934), p. 15. [Typewritten MS.]

[93] *Ibid.*, p. 165.

[94] Dr. Hessler believes that Swift was interested in the Opposition by Pope in 1726, but did not contribute much to the serious literature of the group. (*Op. cit.*, pp. 35, 38.)

[95] *The Poems of Jonathan Swift,* III, 1114. See above, pp. 13–14.

[96] It is interesting to note that the third edition of Defoe's biography of Wild appeared on June 12.

[97] M. D. Hessler, *op. cit.*, p. 5.

[98] As John Edwin Wells points out, "Throughout nearly twenty years preceding the appearance of *Jonathan Wild,* at least from 1725 to 1742, the Great Man in England was Robert Walpole. . . . The mere mention of 'great man' directed the reader's . . . attention to Robert Walpole." ("Fielding's Political Purpose in *Jonathan Wild,*" *PMLA,* XXVIII [1913], 14.)

[99] No. 7.

[100] *Ibid.*

[101] No. 8.

[102] *Ibid.*

[103] M. D. Hessler, *op. cit.*, p. 15.

[104] *Notes and Queries,* 11 series, II (October 1, 1910), 261–63.

[105] *Ibid.*, 12 series, II (December 2, 1916), 441–43.

[106] See also *ibid.*, 12 series, III, 38–39, 74, 237–38.

[107] *Miscellanies,* I, xvii.

[108] According to a note in *The Flying Post; or, The Weekly Medley* for January 11, 1728/29, Gay met Wild by accident at an installment at Windsor. Finding him affable and disposed to talk about his profession, Gay developed a familiarity with him and thereby gained a direct knowledge of "all the knavish Practices and Intrigues of the thieving trade. . . . " (See J. R. Sutherland, *"The Beggar's Opera,"* *TLS* [April 25, 1935], p. 272.) It is possible, of course, that this account is merely another of the numerous attempts to discredit Gay's character by exposing him as an intimate of thieves and rogues.

[109] No. 85 (February 17, 1727/28).

[110] Act I, scene 1.

[111] *Ibid.* The satiric value of having a knave condemn himself out of his own mouth has already been noted. See above, p. 19.

[112] See above, p. 15.

[113] Act I, scene 2.

[114] *Ibid.* See above, p. 7.

[115] Act I, scene 3. See above, pp. 5–6. See also W. E. Schultz, *Gay's Beggar's Opera* . . . p. 174.

[116] Mr. and Mrs. Peachum are happy in being only informally married: "PEACHUM. Do you think your Mother and I should have liv'd comfortably so long together, if ever we had been married?" (Act I, scene 8.) It would be possible to see in this a parallel to Jonathan Wild's known indifference to the marriage ceremony. (See Daniel Defoe, *The Life and Actions of Jonathan Wild*, pp. 257–58.)

[117] Act I, scene 4.

[118] Act I, scene 8. See above, p. 21.

[119] Act III, scene 5. See above, p. 5. Note that Gay's first meeting with Jonathan Wild occurred, supposedly, at an installment at Windsor. (See note 108.)

[120] Act I, scene 11.

[121] Act II, scene 5.

[122] Act III, scene 11. This, incidentally, is Peachum's final speech.

[123] W. E. Schultz states that the lovers were largely responsible for making attendance at *The Beggar's Opera* the modish thing. (*Op. cit.*, p. 13.)

[124] For a summary of this subject, see W. E. Schultz, *op. cit.*, pp. 178–97; Edmund M. Gagey, *Ballad Opera* (1937), pp. 45–46; and D. H. Stevens, "Some Immediate Effects of *The Beggar's Opera*," in *The Manly Anniversary Studies* . . . (1923), pp. 180–89.

[125] *The Intelligencer*, No. III [May 25, 1729], in *The Prose Works of Jonathan Swift, D. D.*, ed. by Temple Scott (1902), IX, 321. Denying that their observations applied to the present time was, of course, one of the commonest evasions of Opposition writers.

[126] This device was also used, later in 1728, by Thomas Walker, the original actor of Macheath, who put together *The Quaker's Opera*, which was acted at Lee's and Harper's Great Theatrical Booth at Bartholomew Fair and was printed after a very short run. This play is a poor fusion of *The Beggar's Opera* and *The Prison-Breaker*, which includes an offensive old Quaker among its characters. Jonathan Wild appears again, virtually unchanged, as Jonathan Wile. (See A. Nicoll, *A History of Early Eighteenth Century Drama* . . . p. 244.)

[127] See M. D. Hessler, *op. cit.*, p. 10.

[128] No. 87 (March 2, 1727/28).

[129] No. 97 (May 11, 1728).

[130] No. 320 (August 19, 1732).

[131] *The Craftsman*, V (1729), 315.

[132] "Bob Screen" was one of the Opposition's numerous nicknames for Walpole. See M. D. Hessler, *op. cit.*, p. 19.

[133] See Sir John Morley, *Walpole* in *The Works of Lord Morley* (1921), XIII, 226–27.

[134] No. 825 (April 24, 1742), reprinted in *The Gentleman's Magazine*, XII, 201.

[135] No. 856 (November 20, 1742), reprinted in *The Gentleman's Magazine*, XII, 593. The joining of Wild's name to Cromwell's is an instance of the comparison of a criminal and a conqueror. The similarity which many eighteenth century moralists saw between criminals and conquerors will receive considerable attention in another part of this study.

[136] This group had as its figurehead Frederick, Prince of Wales, who was interested

in the Opposition as early as 1729, and became its acknowledged leader in 1736. According to Patriot writers, Frederick embodied "the abstract idea of public spirit and patriotism, which the Opposition had all along contrasted with their picture of Walpole's corrupt government. . . ." (M. D. Hessler, *op. cit.,* pp. 71–72. See also M. H. Cable, "The Idea of a Patriot King in the Propaganda of the Opposition to Walpole, 1735–1739," *PQ,* XVIII [April, 1939], 119–30.) It is well known that Fielding greatly admired Chesterfield and Lyttelton, and particularly the latter, who proved himself both friend and benefactor. Dr. Hessler states that after the Licensing Act forced Fielding from the theatre, he "began, apparently at once, to write for *Common Sense.* . . ." (M. D. Hessler, *op. cit.,* p. 171.)

[137] *Common Sense,* I (1738), [Sig. A₄].

[138] *Ibid.,* pp. 185–88.

[139] *Ibid.*

[140] Vol. II (1739), 275.

[141] *Ibid.,* p. 279.

[142] The temptation to believe that Fielding wrote this article is a natural one. He was undoubtedly an occasional contributor to *Common Sense* in 1738, and some scholars have conjectured that it was in 1737 or 1738 that Fielding, full of indignation over the Licensing Act, began to write *Jonathan Wild* as an attack on Walpole, who was instrumental in passing the bill. (A. Digeon, *Les Romans de Fielding,* p. 133.) There is, unfortunately, no external evidence to suggest that this sketch of Wild is Fielding's, and evidence provided by style points, if anywhere, away from Fielding.

[143] No. 125, reprinted in *The Scots Magazine,* I (November, 1739), 559.

[144] July 17, 1742, reprinted in *The Gentleman's Magazine,* XII, 364.

[145] No. 52 (December 8, 1733), reprinted in *The Gentleman's Magazine,* III, 639.

[146] "Epilogue to the Satires: Dialogue II," ll. 38–39. There is another reference to Wild in ll. 52–55:

> "P. Must Satire then nor rise nor fall?
> Speak out, and bid me blame no rogues at all.
> E. Yes, strike that Wild, I'll justify the blow.
> P. Strike? why the man was hang'd ten years ago."

[147] See above, p. 19.

[148] Fielding notes that the authenticity of the memoirs which he used "hath been sometimes questioned." See above, p. 24.

[149] *Miscellanies,* I, xvi–xvii. (In references to the first two volumes of the *Miscellanies,* numerals indicate volume and page.) The substance of the part of *The Ordinary of Newgate his Account of the Behaviour, last Dying Speeches and Confessions of the four Malefactors who were Executed at Tyburn . . . the 24th of May, 1725,* which concerns Jonathan Wild is given in *The Political State of Great Britain,* XXIX, 507–10.

[150] III, xiii, 274–75. (Since *Jonathan Wild* is wholly contained in Vol. III of the *Miscellanies,* numerals in references to it signify, respectively, book, chapter, and page.)

[151] See note 36.

[152] IV, i, 293–94.

[153] III, xiv, 275–82, and IV, i, 291–93.

[154] IV, iii, 301–10.

[155] See *The Life and Notorious Transactions of Roger Johnson . . .* p. 25, and *passim.*

[156] IV, xiv, 386–99. The drunkenness and irreligion of the ordinaries of Newgate

was traditional in the eighteenth century. Defoe's Moll Flanders was horrified by the conduct of one: "The ordinary of Newgate came to me, and talked a little in his way, but all his divinity ran upon confessing my crime, as he called it (though he knew not what I was in for), making a full discovery and the like, without which he told me God would never forgive me; and he said so little to the purpose that I had no manner of consolation from him; and then to observe the poor creature preaching confession and repentance to me in the morning, and find him drunk with brandy by noon, this had something in it so shocking, that I began to nauseate the man . . . so that I desired him to trouble me no more." (*The Fortunes and Misfortunes of the Famous Moll Flanders*, ed. by G. H. Maynadier [1903], II, 123.) Fielding accepted apparently without question this general reputation, which in the case of Thomas Purney, who was ordinary at the time of Wild's imprisonment and execution, was not justified. Purney was a gentle and pious young man, something of a pastoral poet, and a critical "prophet of romanticism." (See H. O. White, "Thomas Purney . . ." *Essays and Studies of the English Association*, XV [1929], 67-97.)

According to the version of the ordinary's account given in *The Political State of Great Britain*, Wild does seem to have had a considerable interview with the so-called "Bishop of Newgate," during which the reverend gentleman counseled him to spend less time in asking questions about the other world and more in preparing his soul for eternity. Fielding may well have had this conversation in mind when he wrote the burlesque account in *Jonathan Wild*.

[157] IV, xv, 403-4.

[158] IV, xv, 405-7.

[159] See above, pp. 10-11.

[160] The reference here is to the seven years which many criminals spent in America as slaves on the plantations, as did Defoe's Colonel Jack, for example. This punishment, called "transportation," was usually given to first offenders and petty criminals.

[161] There is much satire on high-life in Fielding's *Jonathan Wild*. It will be discussed in some detail later. See Gerard E. Jensen, "Fashionable Society in Fielding's Time," *PMLA*, XXXI (1916), 79-89.

[162] *Miscellanies*, I, xviii.

[163] See D. H. Stevens, *op. cit.*, p. 188. See also M. D. Hessler, *op. cit.*, pp. 124-50.

[164] M. D. Hessler, *op. cit.*, p. 141.

[165] May 21, 1737. See W. L. Cross, *The History of Henry Fielding*, I, 220-21.

[166] J. E. Wells, "Fielding's Political Purpose in *Jonathan Wild*," *PMLA*, XXVIII (1913), 12.

[167] March 4, 1739/40, in *The Champion*, I (1741), 330.

[168] March 24, 1740/41. Reprinted in M. D. Hessler, *op. cit.*, p. 102. See also J. E. Wells, "The 'Champion' and Some Unclaimed Essays by Henry Fielding," *Englische Studien*, XLVI (1912-13), 355-66.

[169] The "Register of New Publications" in *The Gentleman's Magazine* for July, 1731, contains the following tantalizing entry: "An Answer to one Part of an infamous Libel, reflecting on Captain Vinegar, and the late worthy *Jonathan Wilde* . . . By *Hercules Vinegar*, of *Hockley in the Hole*, Esq. Pr. 6d." A pamphlet on Jonathan Wild written in 1731 by Fielding under the pseudonym "Hercules Vinegar" would be a rare find. J. E. Wells, who was unable to locate a copy, suggests that it was probably a parody of a political pamphlet written during the paper war over William Pulteney. (*The Nation*, XCVI [January 16, 1913], 53-54.) The substitution of rogues for political personages has already been shown to have been a common device in

political satire. The name "Hercules Vinegar," later adopted by Fielding, actually belonged to a well-known boxer. The name was frequently used as a pseudonym by satirists during the 1730s. See J. E. Wells, "Fielding's 'Champion' and Captain Hercules Vinegar," *MLR*, VIII (1913), 165–72.

[170] Aurélien Digeon believes that a desire to experiment in picaresque biography originally impelled Fielding to begin *Jonathan Wild:* "Si l'on faisait sortir de l'ouvrage le premier livre et, dans les autres, les chapitres épars que j'ai énumérés [II, vi; III, iii, vi–ix, xiii, xiv; IV, ii, iii, xiii–xv] il serait à peine besoin de quelques sutures pour en faire un roman se suffisant à lui-même, et qui serait une biographie pure, sobre, et sèche de Jonathan Wild. J'ai la conviction que nous posséderions là la vein primitive, la forme sous laquelle Fielding a d'abord conçu son roman, et probablement la forme sous laquelle il l'a d'abord rédigé." (*Les Romans de Fielding*, p. 146.)

[171] See particularly J. E. Wells, "Fielding's Political Purpose in *Jonathan Wild*," *PMLA*, XXVIII (1913), 1–55; W. L. Cross, *The History of Henry Fielding*, I, 409–10; M. D. Hessler, *op. cit.*, pp. 124–50.

[172] J. E. Wells, "Fielding's Political Purpose in *Jonathan Wild*," p. 7.

[173] M. D. Hessler, *op. cit.*, p. 15.

[174] I, iii, 15.

[175] *Ibid.*

[176] Note that a Robin of Bagshot is included among the characters in *The Beggar's Opera*.

[177] II, v, 138.

[178] I, xiii, 79.

[179] *Ibid.*, p. 81.

[180] II, vi, 140–41. The whole speech is obviously a parody of the high-flown language of political oratory.

[181] *Ibid.*, p. 141.

[182] *Ibid.*, p. 142.

[183] IV, xvi, 413.

[184] I, xiv, 91.

[185] *Ibid.*, pp. 91–92.

[186] IV, iii, 301.

[187] *The History of Henry Fielding*, I, 409.

[188] "Fielding's Political Purpose in *Jonathan Wild*," p. 2.

[189] *DNB*, XVI, 475.

[190] *Ibid.*, III, 1121. Digeon believes that the new Wild represents the Earl of Wilmington, who became First Lord of the Treasury after Walpole's resignation. (*Les Romans de Fielding*, p. 137.) To be sure, Wilmington had on previous occasions disagreed with Walpole. But the characters of Wild and Wilmington are inconsistent. Wild is aggressive and arrogant; Wilmington, even after he entered the cabinet, was generally considered a personal and political cipher. (*DNB*, IV, 906.)

[191] The very grave man who leads the disaffected debtors probably represents William Shippen, an independent and incorruptible old Jacobite who occasionally aligned himself with the Opposition. When the motion against Walpole was introduced in 1741, however, Shippen regarded it as a scheme for turning out one bad minister and bringing in another, and with several of his followers broke with the Opposition. Oddly enough, "honest Shippen" died two weeks after Fielding's *Miscellanies* appeared. (*DNB*, XVIII, 117–18.)

[192] *Miscellanies*, I, xvii.

[193] W. E. Schultz, *op. cit.*, p. 196.

[194] *Miscellanies*, I, xviii.

[195] J. E. Wells, "Fielding's Political Purpose in *Jonathan Wild*," p. 55.

II. THE ETHICAL PROBLEM

[1] I, i, 4–5.

[2] *Miscellanies*, I, xxvi.

[3] *Ibid.*, xxviii.

[4] *The Universal Spectator* . . . I, 238.

[5] *The British Journal*, CCLIII (July 29, 1727).

[6] *The London Journal*, LXXXVII (March 25, 1720).

[7] *The Free Briton*, No. 151 (October 19, 1732), reprinted in *The Gentleman's Magazine*, II, 1013.

[8] *The Whole Duty of Man* . . . (1733), p. 108. The discussion of ambition occurs in the division entitled "Of Contentedness and the Contraries to It."

[9] *New Memoirs of Literature*, III (January, 1726), 259. Saint-Pierre passes judgment on Solon, Epaminondas, Alexander the Great, Scipio Africanus, Julius Caesar, Sulla, Cato, Descartes, Henry IV of France, and Charles V. He puts Alexander and Caesar in the second rank, that occupied by illustrious men. See *Ouvrages de morale et de politique* . . . (1740), XIV, 110–67.

[10] *A Collection of Miscellany Letters, selected out of Mist's Weekly Journal*, I, 257.

[11] *The Englishman* . . . No. 48 (January 23, 1714). See also Isaac Barrow, Sermon LX, "Of Self-Love in General," in *The Theological Works of Isaac Barrow* (1830), III, 353–66. This is the first sermon of a series on the abuses of self-love.

[12] Steele refers to "a Man living, who, from the Thirst of an unjust Fame, has spilt a greater Quantity of the Blood of his Contemporaries than any other of the Sons of *Adam*. . . ." (*The Englishman* . . . No. 48.) This is undoubtedly a bit of Whig war mongering, directed at Louis XIV.

[13] *Ibid.*

[14] See above, pp. 22–31.

[15] *The Craftsman*, No. 220 (September 19, 1730).

[16] *The Statesman's Progress* . . . [1741], pp. 7–13.

[17] No. 12 (May 2, 1718). Walpole began his long career as Prime Minister and Chancellor of the Exchequer in 1721, and an articulate Opposition was not organized until 1726. (M. D. Hessler, *op. cit.*, p. 6.) In an early *Spectator* essay Steele several times refers to noblemen and ministers as "great men," and rallies them on their lofty conduct at levees. (No. 193 [October 11, 1711].) Anti-Walpole satirists did not originate the character of the great man as politician.

[18] See particularly Nos. 81 and 100.

[19] No. 132 (June 26, 1719).

[20] No. 9 (January 2, 1726/27).

[21] *The Craftsman*, No. 2 (December 9, 1726).

[22] See *The Craftsman*, No. 300 (April 15, 1732). See also *The Present State of the Republick of Letters*, III (1729), 218. Charles XII's invasion of Norway in 1716 was by many feared to be the preliminary step to a descent on Scotland. At the time Baron von Görtz was in Holland, procuring money and supposedly carrying on negotiations with Jacobite agents and the Pretender himself. (See *The Cambridge Modern History* [1909], VI, 26–28.)

[23] *The Craftsman*, No. 72 (November 18, 1727).

²⁴ M. D. Hessler, *op. cit.*, p. 19. See *The Craftsman*, Nos. 8, 23, 44, 87, 109.

²⁵ See A. Digeon, *Les Romans de Fielding*, pp. 128-29.

²⁶ *The Free-Thinker*, No. 132.

²⁷ See Sermon XXXV, "Of the Liberty of Moral Agents," in *Sermons on Several Subjects* . . . (1820), II, 5.

²⁸ *Ibid.*, VII, 18.

²⁹ *The Christian Hero* . . . (1725), p. 53.

³⁰ *The London Journal*, No. 653 (January 1, 1731/32).

³¹ No. 320 (August 19, 1732).

³² Sermon LXXXV, "On the Cruelty of Tyrants and their striking Counter-Action by Providence," in *The Works of Thomas Secker, L.L.D.* . . . .(New ed., 1792), II, 512. Francis Hutcheson averred that "the temper of a tyrant seems probably to be a continual state of anger, hatred, and fear," but contended that the tyrant does evil, not out of "disinterested malice," but out of fear of those whom he has harmed. (*An Inquiry into the Original of our Ideas of Beauty and Virtue* . . . [1725], p. 158. This passage occurs in the section headed "Moral Good and Evil.")

³³ See Daniel Defoe's paper on the instability of human glory in *Applebee's Journal* (July 21, 1722), reprinted in W. Lee, *Daniel Defoe* . . . III, 27-30; *The Idea of a Patriot King*, in *The Works of Lord Bolingbroke* (1841), II, 380-90; *Clarissa*, Letter CXXXVI, in *The Works of Samuel Richardson* (1883), VIII, 417; Antoine François Prévost, *The Life and Entertaining Adventures of Mr. Cleveland* (3d ed., 1760), IV, 80-81. The last mentioned work was translated into English immediately after its publication in French in 1732. See James R. Foster, "The Abbé Prévost and the English Novel," *PMLA*, XLII (1927), 448.

³⁴ See *The Present State of the Republick of Letters*, III (January, 1729), 375-79. The article is a review of John Rooke's translation of *Arrian's History of Alexander's Expedition* (1729). In a fulsome dedication to George II Rooke emphasizes the contrast between Alexander's "mistaken Greatness" and George's "real Goodness." (Vol. I, Sig. A₂-A₄.)

³⁵ See for example *The Grubstreet Journal*, No. 114 (March 9, 1732) in *The Gentleman's Magazine*, II, 644.

³⁶ Satire VIII, ll. 97-108, in Nicolas Boileau-Despréaux, *Satires* . . . présenté par Charles-H. Boudhors, *Les Textes français* (1934), p. 59. Other references, characterized by the same acrimony, are to be found in Satire XI, ll. 75-90; and Epîtres I, 8; V, 45-50; IX, 30-34; XI, 30.

³⁷ In "An Enquiry into the Origin of Moral Virtue." See *The Fable of the Bees* . . . [ed.] by F. B. Kaye (1924), I, 55.

³⁸ *An Essay on Man*, Epistle IV, ll. 217-22.

³⁹ See *The Grubstreet Journal*, No. 114.

⁴⁰ See *The Craftsman*, No. 268 (July 21, 1731).

⁴¹ *New Memoirs of Literature*, III, 261.

⁴² *The Spectator*, No. 180 (September 26, 1711). Steele frequently attacked Louis XIV. See for example *The Tatler*, Nos. 19, 23, 24, 26, 29.

⁴³ *Tamerlane; A Tragedy* (5th ed., 1720), Act II, scene 2, p. 3. *Tamerlane* remained more or less in the public eye. Until 1815 it was revived each year on November 5, the anniversary of the arrival of William of Orange.

⁴⁴ *The History of Charles XII, King of Sweden* (6th ed., 1735), p. 25. Elsewhere Voltaire notes that Charles was so enraged by the passage in Boileau's satire in which Alexander is called a fool and a madman that he tore the page from the book (p. 176).

⁴⁵ "Remark O," *The Fable of the Bees* . . . I, 166.

[46] See *New Memoirs of Literature* . . . IV (July, 1726), 349–53. Attributing a prince's faults to his education was not uncommon. Bolingbroke, for instance, in his *Idea of a Patriot King* traced the tyrannical character of Louis XIV to his self-centered education, which was largely in the hands of flatterers. (*The Works of Lord Bolingbroke,* II, 388.)

[47] *The Present State of the Republick of Letters,* IX (1732), 37–60, 182–218.

[48] *History of Charles XII,* pp. 317–18.

[49] *The Vanity of Human Wishes,* ll. 217–20.

[50] See M. H. Cable, *op. cit.,* 123–24.

[51] *The Works of Lord Bolingbroke,* II, 352.

[52] Mallet dedicated *Mustapha* to Frederick, Prince of Wales, the hero of the Patriots.

[53] Lewis N. Chase notes that ambition "is practiced and extolled in the heroic drama [of the late seventeenth century] only by the villains." (*The English Heroic Play* [1903], p. 66.) The Patriot dramas are in several ways linked to the tragedy of the Restoration.

[54] Voltaire writes of Gustavus Vasa: "He was one of those great geniuses, whom nature so rarely forms, and who are born with all the qualifications necessary to govern mankind. . . . His enterprizing genius form'd such designs, as appear rash to the vulgar . . . and which however difficult, his indefatigable courage constantly crown'd with success. He was intrepid with prudence, calm in an age of cruelty, and 'tis said as virtuous as the head of a party can be." (*History of Charles XII,* p. 5.)

[55] Act II, scene 1, p. 15.

[56] *Ibid.,* p. 16.

[57] M. H. Cable states: "Each of these plays includes a character of a wicked minister or favorite. He is a type character, with few or none of the distinguishing features of the satirical portraits in other Opposition propaganda. He is the symbol of a vaguely defined evil called Ministerial Power. Nevertheless, for all his abstractness, he is obviously Walpole, just as the king whom he misleads is obviously George II." (*Op. cit.,* p. 125.)

[58] Other rulers included in the general condemnation of tyrants and conquerors were Tiberius (Francis Atterbury, *Sermons on Several Occasions* [1734], IV, 114; *The Spectator,* No. 408, *A Collection of Miscellany Letters* . . . II, 284); Herod (*The Works of Thomas Secker* . . . II, 512 ff.); Caligula (*The Spectator,* No. 246; *The Theological Works of Isaac Barrow,* III, 369); Domitian (Isaac Barrow, *loc. cit.*); Pompey (*Gulliver's Travels,* Book III, chap. vii; J. Thurmond, *Harlequin Sheppard* . . . p. 5); Sennacherib and Haman (Daniel Waterland, *Sermons on Several Important Subjects* [1776], II, 156); Cato (*The Fable of the Bees* . . . I, 335–36). The list might be greatly extended.

[59] See above, pp. 22–31. One more political reference to the great man as criminal deserves notice here: "*Alexander, Caesar,* and most of the great Conquerors of old, were not better than *Imperial Cut-throats,* or *Banditti,* who robb'd and murther'd in Gangs, too strong to be opposed, and escaped the Gallows, which they deserved, by being above Law." (*The Craftsman,* No. 320 [August 19, 1732].)

[60] See A. Digeon, *Les Romans de Fielding,* p. 128.

[61] Satire XI, ll. 75–79, in *Satires* . . . p. 109.

[62] *The Englishman,* No. 48 (January 23, 1714).

[63] *The London Journal,* LXXXVI (March 18, 1720). The paper referred to is in the form of a letter signed "Jack Ketch," the cant name for the hangman.

[64] Letter LXXXIX, in *A Collection of Miscellany Letters* . . . II, 329.

[65] *Gulliver's Travels,* Book III, chap. vii, in *The Prose Works of Jonathan Swift, D.D.,* VIII, 205.

[66] *Ibid.,* 210.

[67] On the similarity between the great man and the common rogue or criminal, see also *The Statesman's Progress* . . . pp. 7, 13; John Banks, *The Unhappy Favourite; or, The Earl of Essex* (1693), Act III, scene 1, p. 35; *The Universal Spectator,* I, 264; the character Millwood in George Lillo's *The London Merchant* and Mosby in the same dramatist's *Arden of Feversham;* "A Dialogue between Julius Caesar and Jack Sheppard," reprinted in H. Bleackley and S. M. Ellis, *Jack Sheppard* . . . pp. 196-98; J. Thurmond, *op. cit.,* pp. 4-5. See also the discussion in chap. I of the parallel drawn by political satirists between thieves and statesmen. The Opposition writers never tired of this comparison.

[68] For further discussion see Walter Graham, *English Literary Periodicals* (1930), *passim;* Fred O. Nolte, *The Early Middle Class Drama, 1696-1774* (1935), pp. 1-20; Joseph B. Heidler, *The History, from 1700 to 1800, of English Criticism of Prose Fiction* (1928), *passim.*

[69] Charles Whittuck notes that in England the standard of moral excellence was "the good man"; at the same time on the Continent it was the "wise man." (*The "Good Man" of the XVIIIth Century* [1901], p. 3.)

[70] *Ibid.,* pp. 55-63.

[71] *The Gentleman's Magazine,* VIII (January, 1738), 3-4. See also "On Benevolence," *Free Briton,* No. 141 (August 10, 1732) and "Of Friendship and Benevolence," *The London Journal,* No. 720 (April 14, 1733) in *The Gentleman's Magazine,* II, 899 and III, 183-84. For further comment on the good man see R. S. Crane, "Suggestions toward the Genealogy of the Man of Feeling," *ELH,* I (December, 1934), 205-29, and W. Lee Ustick, "Changing Ideals of Aristocratic Character and Conduct in Seventeenth Century England," *MP,* XXX (November, 1932), 147-66. The latter article traces the change, as reflected in the literature of courtesy and conduct, from emphasis on culture and accomplishment to emphasis on goodness and social utility.

[72] In the introduction to *The Moralists* Shaftesbury remarks, "But as low as philosophy is reduced, if morals be allowed belonging to her, politics must undeniably be hers." (*Characteristics* [1900], II, 5.) Edward Bentham is careful to point out that the related subjects of politics and economics "are all of them parts, and very material ones too, of our Moral Conduct." (*An Introduction to Moral Philosophy* [2d ed., 1746], p. 2.) Inclusion of at least a part of politics in the study denoted by the term "ethics" is not, of course, peculiar to the early eighteenth century.

[73] E. Bentham, *op. cit.,* p. 49.

[74] "Of Good Nature in Political Contests," *Free Briton,* No. 203 (October 4, 1733) in *The Gentleman's Magazine,* III, 513.

[75] E. Bentham, *loc. cit.*

[76] *Ibid.*

[77] Sermon XXXVIII, in *Sermons on Several Subjects,* II, 56. Abraham is cited as the finest example of a good man.

[78] Act III, scene vii, p. 47.

[79] *Ibid.,* p. 48.

[80] *The Idea of a Patriot King,* in *The Works of Lord Bolingbroke,* II, 390.

[81] *Ibid.,* p. 376.

[82] See *The Craftsman,* No. 89 (March 16, 1727/28).

[83] See *The History of Charles XII,* p. 153 and *passim.*

[84] *Histoire de l'empire de Russie, sous Pierre-le-Grand* (1835), p. 2.

[85] *New Memoirs of Literature*, III, 259.

[86] *Ibid.*, 261.

[87] See for example *The Spectator*, No. 607 (October 15, 1714).

[88] See C. A. Moore, "Whig Panegyric Verse, 1700–1760," *PMLA*, XLI (June, 1926), 365.

[89] *Tamerlane* [Sig. A₄].

[90] Also included in the roster of good men are Demosthenes, Solon, Scipio Africanus, Cicero, the French kings Louis XII, Francis I, and Henry IV, the Duke of Marlborough, and many others.

[91] *Leviathan* . . . chap. xi, in *The English Works of Thomas Hobbes of Malmesbury* (1839), III, 85–86.

[92] *Ibid.*, chap. vi, p. 51.

[93] Chap. vii, in *The English Works* . . . IV, 53.

[94] Hobbes says, "Desire of office or precedence [is called] Ambition." He goes on to say that this term is commonly used in a condemnatory sense.

[95] "An Enquiry into the Origin of Moral Virtue," in *The Fable of the Bees* . . . I, 41.

[96] *Ibid.*, p. xlvii.

[97] *An Inquiry concerning Virtue or Merit*, Part II, sec. 1, pp. ii and iii, in *Characteristics* . . . II, 282–93.

[98] See *An Inquiry into the Original of our Ideas of Beauty and Virtue* . . . p. 159 and *passim*. Hutcheson believed that evil-doing cannot be separated from self-interest; there is no such passion as "a sedate ultimate desire of the misery of others, when we imagine them no way pernicious to us. . . ." (*Ibid.*, p. 137.)

[99] Sermon XI, "Upon the Love of our Neighbour," in *The Works of Joseph Butler, D.C.L.* . . . (1896), II, 185. See also Leslie Stephen, *History of English Thought in the Eighteenth Century* (1876), II, 55.

[100] Sermon X, "Upon Self-Deceit," *op. cit.*, p. 173.

[101] Sermon XI, *op. cit.*, p. 187.

[102] See A. O. Lovejoy, *The Great Chain of Being* (1936), pp. 200, 203.

[103] *A Treatise of Human Nature* . . . (1896), Book III, sec. III, p. 603.

[104] "Suggestions toward the Genealogy of the Man of Feeling," *ELH*, I (December, 1934), 214. See also the same author's remarks in *PQ*, XI (1932), 203–5, 205–6.

[105] *Ibid.*, p. 222.

[106] "Human Nature," chap. ix, in *The English Works* . . . IV, 49. Earlier in this discourse Hobbes denies the possibility of goodness which is totally divorced from some kind of interest, climaxing his argument with the observation that "even the goodness which we apprehend in God Almighty, is his goodness to us." (Chap. vii, p. 32.)

[107] See Shaftesbury, *An Inquiry* . . . Part II, sec. 2, p. i, in *Characteristics*, II, 308; Joseph Butler, "Preface" [to Sermons preached at the Rolls Chapel], in *Works*, II, 14; E. C. Mossner, *Bishop Butler and the Age of Reason* (1936), pp. 117–18.

[108] See E. C. Mossner, *op. cit.*, pp. 109–16; [C. A. Whittuck], "Self-Love," in *Encyclopædia of Religion and Ethics*, ed. by James Hastings (1921), XI, 359; and J. Butler, *The Analogy of Religion, Natural and Revealed* . . . (1736), 316. It is interesting to note, by way of contrast, the manner in which Hobbes derived conscience from human experience. He says "When two or more men know of one and the same fact, they are said to be 'conscious' of it one to another; which is as much as to know it together. And because such are fittest witnesses of the facts of one another, or of a

third: it was, and ever will be, reputed a very evil act, for any man to speak against his 'conscience' or to corrupt or force another to do so: insomuch that the plea of conscience has always been hearkened unto very diligently in all times. Afterwards men made use of the same word metaphorically, for the knowledge of their own secret facts, and secret thoughts. . . . " (*Leviathan*, I, vii, in *The English Works* . . . III, 7.)

[109] "Shaftesbury and the Ethical Poets in England, 1700–1760," *PMLA*, XXXI (1916), 280.

[110] *The Champion*, January 29, 1739/40. The five Corsican politicians in *The Historical Register*, "the ablest heads in the kingdom, and consequently the greatest men," are distinguished chiefly for their fatuity and venality.

[111] Act I, scene 1. The "comedy" represented is called "The Election."

[112] At the auction which is staged in the second scene of *The Historical Register*, some patriotism and "a curious remnant of political honesty" bring no bid whatever; a thousand pounds, however, is quickly offered for an interest at court.

[113] Admiral Edward Vernon took Porto Bello in the Spanish West Indies late in 1739. He was hailed in England as a hero by all those who wished the navy to revenge Spanish depredations on English commerce. (*DNB*, XX, 268–69.)

[114] See particularly M. D. Hessler, *op. cit.*, pp. 124–50.

[115] See *The Vernoniad* (1741), p. 10n, and *The Champion*, January 3, March 4, and March 27, 1739/40.

[116] *The Champion*, June 10, 1740. Elsewhere Fielding gives as the components of greatness "Pride, Folly, Arrogance, Insolence, and Ill-Nature." ("An Essay on Conversation," in *Miscellanies*, I, 148.)

[117] According to James T. Hillhouse, "The particular quality of character for which heroic playwrights strove was a kind of superhuman greatness both in physical powers and emotion." (*The Tragedy of Tragedies* . . . [1918], p. 33.) In *The Champion* for April 22, 1740, Fielding dwells with contemptuous glee on the absurd actions which Caligula performed to be accounted a hero and a conqueror.

[118] *The Champion*, November 17, 1739. This was the second number of the new periodical. Having introduced the Vinegar family, Fielding is denouncing those who take excessive pride in their ancestry. See also *An Apology for the Life of Mr. T——C——, Comedian* . . . (1740), pp. 81 ff.

[119] *Miscellanies*, I, 328. This dialogue obviously owes a debt to the encounter between Alexander and Diogenes described in the thirteenth of Lucian's *Dialogues of the Dead*. Lucian's attitude toward Alexander is consistently anti-heroic. See *Lucian's Dialogues* . . . translated by Howard Williams (1888), pp. 114–27.

[120] See W. L. Cross, *op. cit.*, I, 284–85. There is a copy of this work, beautifully printed and bound, in the Fielding Collection of Yale University Library.

[121] See A. Digeon, *Les Romans de Fielding*, pp. 129–30.

[122] November 22, 1739. The early essays of *The Champion* are devoted to statements of the periodical's policy.

[123] *Miscellanies*, I, 197–207.

[124] An excerpt from the prologue to *The Coffee-House Politician* is worth quoting as an early statement of ethical principle:

"In ancient Greece, the infant Muse's school,
Where Vice first felt the pen of ridicule,
With honest freedom and impartial blows
The Muse attacked each Vice as it arose:
No grandeur could the mighty villain screen
From the just satire of the comic scene:

No titles could the daring poet cool,
Nor save the great right honourable fool.
They spar'd not even the aggressor's name,
And public villany felt public shame.

. . .

Long hath this gen'rous method been disus'd,
For Vice hath grown too great to be abus'd.

. . .

But the heroic Muse, who sings tonight
Through these neglected tracts attempts her flight."

[125] *Eurydice; A Farce*, in *Miscellanies*, II, 258. Fielding liked to fill his burlesques with farcical statements of serious beliefs. For example, this song from *Tumble-Down Dick; or, Phaeton in the Suds:*

"Great courtiers palaces contain,
Poor courtiers fear a jail;
Great parsons riot in champaign,
Poor parsons sot in ale;
Great whores in coaches gang,
Smaller misses,
For their kisses,
Are in Bridewell bang'd;
Whilst in vogue
Lives the great rogue,
Small rogues are by dozens hang'd."

[126] *Don Quixote in England*, Act II, scene 1.

[127] See G. E. Jensen, "Fashionable Society in Fielding's Time," *PMLA*, XXXI (1916), 79–89. The gist of this article is contained in the following passage: "It was against the vices of the fashionable that Fielding usually directed his criticism. On them he placed responsibility for the general degradation of the age." (Page 79.)

[128] "Of Good Nature," in *Miscellanies*, I, 15.

[129] "An Essay on Conversation," in *Miscellanies*, I, 190.

[130] See *The Champion*, January 24, 1739/40.

[131] *Ibid.*, March 27, 1739/40. In "Of Good Nature" Fielding calls this "the glorious Lust of doing Good."

[132] I, v, 29.

[133] I, xiv, 88–92.

[134] See also I, i, 3, 5–7; I, iii, 15; I, viii, 47–53; I, xiii, 79–82; II, iii, 118; II, iv, 124–28; II, vi, 139–42; II, viii, 155–56; II, xi, 168–69; III, iv, 210–11; III, xiv, 277–80; IV, xiii, 382–84; IV, xvi, 417. In roughly half of these passages Fielding points to the similarity between the statesman and the conqueror and rogue. The great men most frequently mentioned are Alexander and Caesar; others are Charles XII, Louis XIV, Cardinal Wolsey, Nero, and Lysander, the Spartan commander.

[135] I, i, 4.

[136] II, ii, 110.

[137] IV, xvi, 413.

[138] *Ibid.*, p. 409.

[139] *Ibid.*, p. 414.

[140] *Ibid.*, p. 417.

[141] In conversation with the much satirized ordinary of Newgate Heartfree announced *"that he believed a sincere Turk would be saved."* (IV, i, 286.) It is note-

worthy that Parson Adams held the same opinion. (*Joseph Andrews*, Book I, chap. xvii.) Heartfree and the good clergyman have so much in common, indeed, that the former might almost be considered a humorless and imperfect version of the latter.

[142] II, i, 96.

[143] *Ibid.*, p. 98.

[144] J. E. Wells believes that Mrs. Heartfree reflects Charlotte Craddock. ("Fielding's Political Purpose in *Jonathan Wild*," *PMLA*, XXVIII [1913], 2.)

[145] Thomas Davies, "Some Account of the Life of Mr. George Lillo," in *The Works of Mr. George Lillo* . . . (1775), I, xv–xxxv. Davies asserts that Fielding, "our English Cervantes . . . often in his humorous pieces laughed at those ridiculous and absurd criticks who could not possibly understand the merit of BARNWELL [*The London Merchant*] because the subject was low, [and] treated LILLO with great politeness and friendship." (Page xv.)

[146] *The Champion*, February 26, 1739/40. W. L. Cross believes that Fielding was attracted by Lillo's honesty. (*Op. cit.*, III, 266.)

[147] For a complete discussion see C. A. Moore, "Whig Panegyric Verse, 1700–1760," *PMLA*, XLI (1926), 362–401. The general attitude of the poets of commerce can be judged from two stanzas in Edward Young's "Imperium Pelagi; A Naval Lyric":

"Is 'merchant' an inglorious name?
    No; fit for Pindar such a theme;
Too great for me; I pant beneath the weight.
    If loud as Ocean's were my voice,
    If words and thoughts to court my choice
Outnumber'd sands, I could not reach its height.

"Merchants o'er proudest heroes reign;
    Those trade in blessing, these in pain,
At slaughter swell, and shout while nations groan.
    With purple monarchs merchants vie;
    If great to spend, what to supply?
Priests may pray for blessings, merchants pour them down."

(*The Complete Works of the Rev. Edward Young, L.L.D.* . . . [1854], II, 19.) The comparison between the merchant and the conqueror, the traditional hero, is an interesting note.

[148] See G. Hübener, "Der Kaufmann Robinson Crusoe," *Englische Studien*, LIV (1920), 367–98.

[149] Helen Sard Hughes, "The Middle Class Reader and the English Novel," *JEGP*, XXV (1926), 363.

[150] See Hans W. Häusermann, "Aspects of Life and Thought in Robinson Crusoe," *RES*, XI (July and October, 1935), 299–312 and 439–56, particularly 441 ff. Louis B. Wright says, "If one wished to pick a single author in whom the intellectual coming-of-age of the middle class is represented, that author would be Daniel Defoe." (*Middle-Class Culture in Elizabethan England*, [1935], p. 657.)

[151] Act I, scene 1.

[152] Act III, scene 1.

[153] See W. H. Hudson, "George Lillo and 'The London Merchant,' " in *A Quiet Corner in a Library* [1915], pp. 93–162, and J. W. Krutch, *Comedy and Conscience after the Restoration* (1924), *passim*.

[154] H. S. Hughes believes that "it was not accident . . . that the apotheosis of the middle-class hero coincided with the rise of a literary form which treated realistically

common experiences of characters in the middle walks of life. . . . To Defoe, Richardson, and Fielding . . . such a reading-public must have seemed noteworthy. . . ." (*Op. cit.*, p. 364.)

[155] See A. Nicoll, *op. cit.*, p. 124*n.*, and W. L. Cross, *op. cit.*, II, 244-45.

[156] November 17, 1739.

[157] IV, iv, 311-15.

[158] III, x, 255.

[159] II, i, 97.

[160] March 4, 1739/40.

[161] Heartfree is naturally pleased at the prosperous conclusion of events, but even more pleased that his innocence has triumphed over evil. Actually, virtue is its own reward. (IV, xii, 380.)

III. LITERARY FORMS AND TRADITIONS

[1] See F. W. Chandler, *The Literature of Roguery*, I, 143 and *passim*.

[2] The *British Museum Catalogue of Printed Books* lists three execution-day lives of Joseph Blake, six of Jack Sheppard, and eight of Jonathan Wild.

[3] *The Plain Dealer*, LXXX (December 25, 1724). See also Letter LXXXVI, in *A Collection of Miscellany Letters Selected out of Mist's Weekly Journal*, II, 321. The accounts of Paul Lorraine, ordinary of Newgate from 1698 to 1719, became so famous that Pope referred to him as "that great historiographer." (*The Works of Alexander Pope . . .* [1871-89], VII, 67.)

[4] The speech begins: "I know it is the constant custom that those who come to this place should have speeches made for them, and cried about in their own hearing, as they are carried to execution; and truly they are such speeches . . that they would make a man shamed to have such nonsense and false English charged upon him, even when he is going to the gallows." (*The Prose Works of Jonathan Swift . . .* VII, 57. See also XI, 341.)

[5] *The Plain Dealer*, LXXX (December 25, 1724).

[6] A quarter of a century later Francis Coventry, in a dedication addressed to Henry Fielding, observed: "In this *life-writing age* . . . no character is thought too inconsiderable to engage the public notice, or too abandoned to be set up as a pattern of imitation." (*The History of Pompey the Little . . .* [1926], p. 22.)

[7] See F. W. Chandler, *op. cit.*, I, 139.

[8] See for example *A Narrative of All the Robberies, Escapes, &c, of John Sheppard*, in *Romances and Narratives of Daniel Defoe*, XVI, 213. In the Preface to *Lives of the Most Remarkable Criminals . . .* (1874), the collector, who was undoubtedly the author, speaks with pride of the "quantities of expression and minuteness of detail which attest their truth." (I, 1.)

[9] See *A Complete History . . . of the Most Notorious Highwaymen . . .* (1926), pp. 8 ff. Moll Cutpurse's epitaph, according to Smith's account, was composed by none other than "the ingenious Mr. Milton." (Page 290.)

[10] See Jonathan Swift, *op cit.*, VII, 57.

[11] See Mark Longaker, *op. cit.*, p. 128.

[12] See Joseph B. Heidler, *The History, from 1700 to 1800, of English Criticism of Prose Fiction* (1928), pp. 23-35, and Arthur J. Tieje, "The Expressed Aim of the Long Prose Fiction from 1579 to 1740," *JEGP*, XI (1912), 402-32.

[13] *Lives of the Most Remarkable Criminals . . .* I, 267-68. In another life the author,

having described the spiritual misery of criminals, observes: "Guilt is a Companion which never suffers Rest to enter any Bosom where it Inhabits." (*Ibid.*, p. 476.)

[14] See above, pp. 16–19. In the Preface to his *True and Genuine Account of the Life and Actions of Jonathan Wild* . . . Defoe mentions with disapproval those authors who "make a jest of his story, or present his history . . . in a style of mockery and ridicule . . ." (*Romances and Narratives of Daniel Defoe*, XVI, 236.) Aurélien Digeon explains the mocking attitude as a means of taking revenge on criminals for having feared them. (*Les Romans de Fielding*, p. 126.)

[15] See H. Bleackley and S. M. Ellis, *Jack Sheppard* . . . p. 196. In a similar spirit Samuel Butler wrote a "Burlesque Pindarick Ode, to the Memory of the Most Renown'd Claud DuVal, the Highwayman." This elaborate piece of mockery praises DuVal for his genteel manners in robbing, for his gallantry to the ladies, and for his graceful behavior when he was hanged. See *The Posthumous Works of Mr. Samuel Butler* . . . (6th ed., 1754), pp. 45–50.

[16] See F. W. Chandler, *op. cit.*, I, 181.

[17] Ernest A. Baker asserts that the central figure in each of Defoe's low-life narratives is the victim of some social injustice. He concludes that Defoe was preaching "the social lesson of self-help." ("Defoe as a Sociological Novelist," *The Academy*, LXX [May 26, 1906], 502–3.)

[18] Speaking of *Moll Flanders*, F. W. Chandler says: "No doubt he thought less of character-development as such than of the moral influence that his tract might exert upon discouraged thieves condemned to transportation; but his achievement was a long step in advance." (*Op. cit.*, I, 289.) See also Charlotte E. Morgan, *The Rise of the Novel of Manners* . . . (1911), pp. 47, 129–30.

[19] See E. M. Gagey, *Ballad Opera* (1937), pp. 42, 77, 135.

[20] W. M. Dixon notes an intermediate adaptation made late in the seventeenth century by Thomas Betterton. This version was entitled simply *The Revenge; or, The Match in Newgate*. (*CHEL*, VI, 53.)

[21] Act I, scene 1, p. 5. Vizard vaguely resembles the character Cocledemoy in Marston's drama. Cocledemoy, described in the dramatis personae as "a knavishly witty City Companion," is indeed a knave, but not a philosophical one.

[22] Act I, scene 1, p. 4.

[23] The prologue to *Love and Revenge* acknowledges the debt to Marston and Bullock. It is worth nothing that Heartfree, like Mr. Thinkwell of *A Woman's Revenge*, is a loving and generous father who would not have his daughter marry against her wishes. (Act I, scene 4, p. 19.) *Love and Revenge* was itself altered and published in 1742 as *The Bilker Bilk'd; or, A Banquet of Wiles* in a collection of drolls called *The Stroler's Pacquet Opened*. (E. M. Gagey, *op. cit.*, p. 226.) Other low-life dramas which contain anti-heroical sentiments and satire on high-life are: Richard Brome, *A Jovial Crew; or, The Merry Beggars* (1684); *The Prison-Breaker* . . . (1725); Thomas Odell, *The Patron* . . . (1729) and *The Footman* . . . (1732); *The Harlot's Progress* (1733); *The Decoy* (1733); and *The Rival Milliners* (1736). See E. M. Gagey, *op. cit.*, pp. 66–77; and Marie Pabisch, *Picaresque Dramas of the 17th and 18th Centuries*, (1909), pp. 92–93.

[24] Charlotte Morgan labels this spirit "anti-romance," and divides it into three types of expression: the comic romance, the picaresque miscellany, and the general satire. (*Op. cit.*, p. 43.)

[25] *Romances of Roguery* . . . (1899), p. 48.

[26] For a more complete analysis of the basic picaresque character, see F. W. Chandler, *Romances of Roguery* . . . pp. 43–59, and *The Literature of Roguery* . . . I, 1–5.

[27] *Romances of Roguery* . . . p. 48.

[28] [Mateo Alemán], *The Rogue; or, The Life of Guzmán de Alfarache* . . . (1924), III, 338. This edition follows James Mabbe's translation, which was published in 1623.

[29] *The Cheats of Scapin*, Act I, scene 1, in *The Works of Thomas Otway* . . . (1932), I, 295. Otway's adaptation (1676) of Molière's *Les Fourberies de Scapin* remained popular for many years.

[30] Alain-René Le Sage, *The Adventures of Gil Blas de Santillana*, trans. by Tobias Smollett [1907], I, 28.

[31] [Richard Head and Francis Kirkman], *The English Rogue; Described in the Life of Meriton Latroon, a Witty Extravagant* (1665–74), II, 51. *The English Rogue* can scarcely be called a picaresque tale. It is rather a compendium of the roguish tricks and jests recounted in Spanish, French, and English sources. The biographical framework is so casual as to be almost non-existent.

[32] The fact that three English writers of rogue literature—Stevens, Smith, and Johnson—all entitled themselves "Captain" doubtless has some amusing explanation which is now obscured.

[33] There is a temptation to regard Defoe's own contributions to criminal biography as the embryos of his longer narratives, but known chronology does not permit. Nor is it possible to derive his use of the biographical framework from picaresque fiction. Prose fiction before Defoe and for some time after was conventionally fitted into a biographical mold.

[34] Quevedo's "First Vision of the Algouazil (or Catchpole) possest" draws a long comparison between that worthy and a devil, to the latter's advantage. See *The Visions of Dom Francisco de Quevedo Villegas* . . . Made English by Sir Roger L'Estrange (1696), pp. 3–10.

[35] Luke Hutton was a highwayman and pamphleteer who was hanged at York in 1598. In *The Blacke Dogge of Newgate*, following an elaborate metaphor, he presents the thief-taker as a sinister and symbolic black dog:

> "In shape, in nature man, yet men's confusion;
> A madding cur who doth from kind regress;
> A mother's son, and most for to be wondered
> Of mother's sons this dog has spoiled a hundred."

Appended to the poetical sketch is a prose explanation in which thief-taking is revealed as a devilish kind of cony-catching. See A. V. Judges [ed.], *The Elizabethan Underworld* (1930), pp. 265–91, particularly p. 276.

[36] The fact that the picaresque tale was uninfluenced by criminal biography or low-life writings can be explained by chronology. The rogue story was the oldest of these forms and, after reaching its culmination in Le Sage's *Gil Blas* (1715–35) practically ceased to exist as a pure type.

[37] H. K. Banerji believes that this mock genealogy satirizes William Musgrave's *Brief and True History of Robert Walpole and His Family* (1738). (*Henry Fielding, Playwright, Journalist, and Master of the Art of Fiction* [1929], p. 159.) Musgrave also wrote *Genuine Memoirs of the Life and Character of . . . Sir Robert Walpole . . .* (1732).

[38] In one pronouncement Fielding says: "It is most certain that truth is to be found only in the works of those who celebrate the lives of great men, and are commonly called biographers, as the others [historians of countries and the like] should indeed be termed topographers or chorographers. . . ." (*Joseph Andrews*, Book III, chap. i.) Fielding's theory of history was, of course, not entirely original. See for example, Joseph Addison, *The Free-holder* . . . Nos. 35 and 51 (April 20 and June 15, 1716);

The Guardian, No. 25 (April 9, 1713); D. Defoe, *The Life of Colonel Jack,* in *Novels and Miscellaneous Works of Daniel Defoe* (1912), I, 541.

[39] See George Kitchin, *A Survey of Burlesque and Parody in English* (1931), pp. 166–70; F. W. Chandler, *The Literature of Roguery,* I, 303; Mark Longaker, *English Biography in the Eighteenth Century,* p. 152; A. Digeon, *Les Romans de Fielding,* pp. 123–24; and Waldo H. Dunn, *English Biography* (1916), p. 100.

[40] For a further discussion of this point of structure see W. L. Cross, *op. cit.,* II, 161, 179.

[41] See [Anon.], *The History of the Press Yard* . . . (1717), pp. 8, 45–49, 50–51; *The Prison-Breaker* . . . Act I, scene 1; Bernard Mandeville, *An Enquiry into the Causes of the Frequent Executions at Tyburn* . . . pp. 19–46; and Luke Owen Pike, *A History of Crime in England* . . . (1876), II, *passim.* Francis Coventry, one of Fielding's admirers, praises him for his "thorough Insight into Low-life," but does not expand his assertion. See *An Essay on the New Species of Writing Founded by Mr. Fielding* . . . (1751), p. 29.

[42] Horace Bleackley asserts that Fireblood represents Fielding's portrait of Jack Sheppard, but offers no satisfactory support for his statement. (*Op. cit.,* pp. 76–77.) Roger Johnson, who appears in IV, iii, is omitted from this list because he is simply an instrument of political satire.

[43] H. K. Banerji sees significance in the fact that the names Straddle and Bagshot occur in *The Beggar's Opera* and in *Jonathan Wild.* (*Op. cit.,* p. 157.) Although this fact is itself of minor importance, one nevertheless suspects that Fielding owed more to *The Beggar's Opera* than to any other piece of low-life writing.

[44] In a generally bitter "Modern Glossary" Fielding later defined marriage as "A Kind of Traffic carried on between the two Sexes, in which both are constantly endeavouring to cheat each other, and both are commonly Losers in the End." (*The Covent-Garden Journal,* No. 4 [January 14, 1752].)

[45] I, iii, 19. Scapin, of course, represents the *gracioso,* dramatic brother to the *picaro.* See F. W. Chandler, *Romances of Roguery,* p. 367.

[46] This view directly opposes that of A. Digeon, who holds that *Jonathan Wild* cannot be understood without reference to the picaresque tradition. (*Les Romans de Fielding,* p. 119.)

[47] *The Literature of Roguery,* I, 306.

[48] George Sherburn believes that *Amelia* is not so much a comic epic as a serious epic in prose. ("Fielding's *Amelia;* An Interpretation," *ELH,* III [March, 1936], 2.) James Beattie says in his essay "On Poetry and Music": "Of the Comic Epopee we have two exquisite Models in English, I mean the *Amelia* and *Tom Jones* of Fielding." (*Essays* . . . [1776], p. 428*n.*) It is odd that Beattie should have omitted mention of *Joseph Andrews,* the work to which Fielding most explicitly attached the label "comic epic poem in prose."

[49] For an exhaustive study of the critical background of these theories see Ethel M. Thornbury, *Henry Fielding's Theory of the Comic Prose Epic* (1931).

[50] *Ibid.,* p. 98. Among the eighteenth-century translators were Thomas Parnell, Samuel Wesley, and James Ralph, one of Fielding's literary associates.

[51] J. E. Spingarn, *A History of Literary Criticism in the Renaissance,* (1899), pp. 31, 36. One is tempted to conjecture that Homer's lost *Margites* was a kind of comic epic. Aristotle said of it: "As in the serious style, Homer is pre-eminent among poets . . . so he too first laid down the main lines of Comedy. . . . His Margites bears the same relation to Comedy that the Iliad and Odyssey do to Tragedy." (*Poetics* iv, in S. H. Butcher, *Aristotle's Theory of Poetry and Fine Art* . . . [1911], p. 17.) Field-

ing apparently accepted this hypothesis. In the Preface to *Joseph Andrews* he writes: "The EPIC, as well as the DRAMA, is divided into tragedy and comedy. HOMER, who was the father of this species of poetry, gave us a pattern of both of these, though that of the latter kind is entirely lost. . . . "

[52] See E. M. Thornbury, *op. cit.*, pp. 54–64.

[53] *Joseph Andrews* was published before *Jonathan Wild,* which made up the third volume of the *Miscellanies.* Certain scholars—Edmund Gosse, Austin Dobson, F. W. Chandler, and Aurélien Digeon among them—have held that, despite this fact of chronology, *Jonathan Wild* must have been completed, or at least substantially written, before Fielding finished *Joseph Andrews.* Some even give 1737, the year of the Licensing Act, as the time when Fielding began his life of the great rogue. Other students, notably W. L. Cross, argue that such subjective dating is motivated by an effort to see in Fielding's career a steady and consistent development. Proof that *Jonathan Wild,* which as a comic prose epic is less complete and true to form than *Joseph Andrews,* antedates the latter work would add an agreeable neatness to the present case, but would not actually alter it.

[54] See E. M. Thornbury, *op. cit.*, p. 50, and J. B. Heidler, *op. cit.*, p. 47. Some critics, naturally, made a sharp distinction between epic and romance. These men, says W. P. Ker, "were generally right in distinguishing between Epic and Romance, and generally wrong in separating the one kind from the other as opposite and mutually exclusive forms, instead of seeing with Tasso, in his critical discourses, that romance may be included in epic." (*Epic and Romance* . . . [1922], p. 31.)

[55] See George Sherburn, *op. cit.*

[56] E. M. Thornbury in defining the term *fable* makes this statement: "The fable is an abstract summary of the moral, and may be compared, says Le Bossu, to the fables of Aesop." (*Op. cit.*, p. 60.) Dr. Johnson defines the word in its epic sense thus: "The series or contexture of events which constitute a poem epic or dramatick."

[57] See George Sherburn, *op. cit.*, pp. 3–4.

[58] It is worth noting that Le Bossu, the chief critical authority for the prose epic, stated that it is not necessary that the hero of a poem be a virtuous man. See J. B. Heidler, *op. cit.*, p. 41.

[59] In the previous section considerable attention was given to the symbolization of Wild and Heartfree. Some remarks of S. H. Butcher on characters in comedy provide incidental illumination here: "In respect of character-drawing, its [comedy's] usual method . . . is to embody a dominant characteristic or a leading passion so that the single attribute becomes the man. A character so created . . . almost of necessity runs to caricature. It is framed on lines of impossible simplicity. . . . " (*Op. cit.*, pp. 385–86.)

[60] Dr. Johnson defines "sentiment" thus: "The sense considered distinctly from the language or things; a striking sentence [i.e., maxim] in a composition."

[61] IV, xvi, 413.

[62] II, iv, 125–26.

[63] III, v, 215.

[64] Fielding nowhere directly defines "burlesque" in relation to diction. It seems safe to apply to the term in that reference Fielding's general definition of the burlesque as "what is monstrous and unnatural."

[65] I, xiv, 84–85.

[66] I, x, 62. At this point Fielding virtually underlines his ludicrous use of heroic epithet. Having revealed Laetitia's passion for Tom Smirk, Fielding, with feigned

sorrow, remarks: "the FAIR *Laetitia* (for we must, in this single Instance, imitate *Virgil*, where he drops the *pius* and the *pater*, and drop our favorite Epithet of *chaste*) the FAIR *Laetitia* had, I say, made *Smirk* as happy as *Wild* desired to be. . . . "

[67] Le Sage's *Gil Blas,* a work which Fielding admired, includes many life-stories. The most entertaining are those of Doña Mencia of Mosquera, of Don Alphonso and the Fair Seraphina, of Laura, and of Scipio. *Gil Blas* is basically a picaresque tale, but so complicated and elevated that it resembles a comic romance.

[68] IV, vii, viii, ix, x, xii.

[69] IV, ix, 346–52 Fielding had announced in his Preface to the *Miscellanies* that one chapter was intended as ridicule of the extravagant accounts of travelers. (*Miscellanies,* I, xxiv.) Although there is some similarity between these chapters and Defoe's *Captain Singleton,* it is not likely that Fielding aimed his satire at any particular travel tale.

[70] It is worth noting that a virtuous woman's resistance is a minor event in Le Sage's *Bachelier de Salamanque* and a major theme in *Le Philosophe anglais; histoire de Cléveland,* by the Abbé Prévost. In the latter work Gelin persuades Mme Cléveland that Cléveland has been unfaithful and that elopement with him is her best escape from an intolerable situation. They sail for Spain, but Gelin keeps her on the high seas for a long time and makes repeated advances. Mme Cléveland never yields, and shortly after their arrival at Corunna escapes from her would-be seducer. See *Oeuvres choisies de l'Abbé Prévost* (1783), VI, 141–324 [Book IX]. Fielding undoubtedly knew the work of the Abbé Prévost. It is possible, as A. Digeon suggests, that in these chapters of attempted seduction he was parodying not only *Pamela,* but also a number of other extravagant accounts "sans intention particulière." (*Les Romans de Fielding,* p. 148n.) The motif of defense against seduction is, amusingly enough, the center of the Spanish *novela, La Picara Justina,* a work whose gross frankness would probably have shocked Samuel Richardson out of existence. Justina, a country wench, repels all assaults and in the end triumphantly marries a gentleman. "Captain" John Stevens translates this *novela* under the title, *The Country Jilt.* See *The Spanish Libertines . . .* (1707), pp. 1–65.

[71] Certain scholars have severely censured Fielding for inserting Mrs. Heartfree's pedestrian narrative just as the history of Wild is reaching its climax. G. T. Bispham, for example, writes: "In point of style, *Jonathan Wild* may challenge comparison with any masterpiece of prose satire. I would write with the same praise of its structure, were it not for the long interruption in the story caused by Mrs. Heartfree's recital of her adventures by sea and land. . . . It adds no new thing to the purpose of that satire. Evil has been sufficiently unmasked in all its ugliness. The least sensitive reader grows disgusted and weary at a new succession of villainies. . . . The time for light mocking is passed." ("Fielding's *Jonathan Wild,*" in *Eighteenth Century Literature, an Oxford Miscellany* [1909], p. 71, by permission of The Clarendon Press, Oxford.) See also H. K. Banerji, *op. cit.,* p. 162.

Bispham and the others err in insisting that Fielding should have observed a rule of structure which did not exist in his time. Novels were still fundamentally chronological narratives. The well-made novel, like the well-made play, is a later creation.

[72] E. M. Thornbury, *op. cit.,* p. 110.

[73] VIII, i.

[74] II, xiii, 179.

[75] See also *Tom Jones,* Book IX, chap. i.

[76] *Characteristics,* I, 85. In an essay obviously indebted to Shaftesbury's, Anthony

Collins defends the use of ridicule and irony in divine controversy by demonstrating that they have been among the most effective weapons of the Established Church against its enemies. (*A Discourse Concerning Ridicule and Irony in Writing* . . . [1729], p. 7 and *passim*.)

[77] *Reflexions upon Ridicule* (4th ed., 1727), I, 58.

[78] September 3, 1737.

[79] John W. Draper, "The Theory of the Comic in Eighteenth-Century England," *JEGP*, XXXVII (1938), 221. See also *The Spectator*, No. 249 [Addison], and William Whitehead, "On Ridicule" [1743], in *The Works of the English Poets* . . . (1810), XVII, 206–8.

[80] An excellent example of the affectation which springs from vanity is to be found in Ragotin, the proud and irascible dwarf of Scarron's *Roman comique*. Ragotin is introduced in these words: "Among the rest appeared a little man, who was a widower, a lawyer by profession, and an officer in a small court of judicature in the neighborhood. Since the death of his little wife, he sometimes threatened the women to marry again, and sometimes the clergy of the province to turn priest, nay even preaching prelate. He was the greatest little fool that ever ran madding about since Orlando Furioso. He had studied books all his lifetime; but though the chief end of scholarship is knowledge of truth, yet was he as great a liar as a page, proud and obstinant as a pedant, and so bad a poet as to deserve drowning. . . . " (*The Comical Romance* . . . [1892], I, 30.) Ragotin is ridiculous, not because he is a dwarf, but because he strives to be the cavalier.

[81] IV, xvi, 410.

[82] *Miscellanies*, I, xxx.

[83] See above, p. 94.

[84] III, iv, 211, 213.

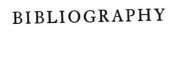

BIBLIOGRAPHY

BIBLIOGRAPHY

THIS BIBLIOGRAPHY contains works of direct and of tangential importance to the subject. It is by no means complete. For the best available critical bibliography of Fielding's works see W. L. Cross, *The History of Henry Fielding,* III, 289–366.

Addison, Joseph. The Free-holder; or, Political Essays [1715–16]. London, Jacob and Richard Tonson, 1758.

Adlerfeld, Gustavus. The Military History of Charles XII, King of Sweden. . . . Translated into English [by Henry Fielding]. 3 volumes. London, J. and P. Knapton, A. Millar, and J. Nourse, 1740.

Alden, Raymond. The Rise of Formal Satire in England under Classical Influence. Philadelphia, University of Pennsylvania, 1899.

[Alemán, Mateo]. The Rogue; or, The Life of Guzmán de Alfarache . . . Done into English by James Mabbe, *anno* 1623. 4 volumes. London, Constable and Co., 1924.

Ames, John G. The English Literary Periodical of Morals and Manners. Mt. Vernon, Ohio, Republican Publishing Co., 1904.

[Anonymous]. An Authentick Narrative of the Life and Actions of Jonathan Wild (Citizen and Thief-Taker of London. . .). 2d edition. London, A. Moore, 1725.

——— A Full and Particular Account of the Life and Notorious Transactions of Roger Johnson . . . to the Time of His Death. London, C. Corbett, 1740.

——— The History of the Press Yard. . . . London, T. Moor, 1717.

——— Love and Revenge; or, The Vintner Outwitted: An Opera. London, J. Clark, 1729.

——— News from the Dead; or, A Dialogue between Blueskin, Shepperd, and Jonathan Wild. London, J. Thompson [1725].

——— The Prison-Breaker; or, The Adventures of John Sheppard. . . . London, 1725.

——— The Statesman's Progress; or, A Pilgrimage to Greatness, by John Bunyan [1741]. Edinburgh, The Aungerville Society, 1886.

——— Weighley, alias Wild. London, J. Roberts, 1725.

——— The Whole Duty of Man Laid Down in a Plain and Familiar Way for the Use of all, but Especially the Meanest Reader . . . [1658]. London, John Eyre, 1733.

Arrian's History of Alexander's Expedition, Translated from the Greek
... by Mr. [John] Rooke. 2 volumes. London, T. Worrall, 1729.

Atterbury, Francis. Sermons on Several Occasions. London, George
James, 1734.

Aydelotte, Frank. Elizabethan Rogues and Vagabonds, in Oxford Historical and Literary Studies, Vol. I. Oxford, Clarendon Press, 1913.

Baker, Ernest A. "Defoe as a Sociological Novelist," The Academy,
LXX (May 26, 1906), 502–3.

Banerji, H. K. Henry Fielding, Playwright, Journalist, and Master of
the Art of Fiction. Oxford, Basil Blackwell, 1929.

Banks, John. The Unhappy Favourite; or, The Earl of Essex.... London, Richard Bentley, 1693.

Barker, Richard H. Mr. Cibber of Drury Lane. New York, Columbia
University Press, 1939.

[Barrow, Isaac]. The Theological Works of Isaac Barrow, D.D. Oxford,
Oxford University Press, 1830.

Bateson, F. W. English Comic Drama, 1700–1750. Oxford, Clarendon
Press, 1929.

Beattie, James. Essays.... Edinburgh, William Creech, 1776.

Beatty, Richard C. "Criticism in Fielding's Novels...." PMLA, XLIX
(1934), 1087–1100.

Beljame, Alexandre. Le Public et les hommes des lettres en Angleterre
aux dix-huitième siècle. 2d edition. Paris, Librairie Hachette, 1897.

Bentham, Edward. An Introduction to Moral Philosophy. 2d edition.
Oxford, James Fletcher, 1746.

Bernbaum, Ernest. The Drama of Sensibility.... Boston, Ginn and Co.,
1915.

Bispham, G. T. "Fielding's Jonathan Wild," in Eighteenth Century
Literature; An Oxford Miscellany. Oxford, Clarendon Press, 1909.

Bissell, Frederick Olds. Fielding's Theory of the Novel. Ithaca, New
York, Cornell University Press, 1933.

Blanchard, Frederic T. Fielding the Novelist. . . . New Haven, Yale
University Press, 1926.

Bleackley, Horace, and S. M. Ellis. Jack Sheppard. . . . Edinburgh and
London, William Hodge and Co. [1933].

Boileau-Despréaux, Nicolas. Satires ... présenté par Charles-H. Boudhors. Les Textes français, Paris, Société des Belles Lettres, 1934.

Bond, Richmond P. English Burlesque Poetry, 1700–1750. Cambridge,
Harvard University Press, 1932.

Borrow, George. Celebrated Trials and Remarkable Cases of Criminal
Jurisprudence ... [1825]. London, Jonathan Cape [1928].

British Journal, The. London, Nos. 1–277, September 22, 1722—January, 1728.

Brooke, Henry. Gustavus Vasa; The Deliverer of His Country. London, R. Dodsley, 1739.

Bullock, [Christopher]. A Woman's Revenge; or, A Match in Newgate. London, E. Curll, 1715.

Burch, Charles E. "The Moral Elements in Defoe's Fiction," *The London Quarterly and Holborn Review,* 6 series, VI (April, 1937), 207–13.

Butcher, S. H. Aristotle's Theory of Poetry and Fine Art, with a Critical Text and Translation of the Poetics. 4th edition. London, Macmillan & Co., Ltd., 1911.

Butler, Joseph. The Analogy of Religion, Natural and Revealed, to the Constitution and Course of Nature. London, James, John, and Paul Knapton, 1736.

————— The Works of Joseph Butler, D.C.L. . . . Edited by W. E. Gladstone. 2 volumes. Oxford, Clarendon Press, 1896.

[Butler, Samuel]. The Posthumous Works of Mr. Samuel Butler. 6th edition. London, Richard Baldwin, 1754.

Byrom, John. Miscellaneous Poems. 2 volumes. Manchester, J. Harrop, 1773.

Cable, M. H. "The Idea of a Patriot King in the Propaganda of the Opposition to Walpole, 1735–1739," *PQ,* XVIII (April, 1939), 119–30.

Cambridge History of English Literature, The. Edited by A. W. Ward and A. R. Waller. New York, G. P. Putnam's Sons [1907–1916].

Cambridge Modern History, The. Edited by A. W. Ward, G. W. Prothero, and Stanley Leathes. New York, Macmillan Co., 1909.

Campbell, R. The London Tradesman. London, T. Gardner, 1747.

Cervantes Saavedra, Miguel de. Don Quixote. Translated by Charles Jervas [1742]; edited by James Fitzmaurice-Kelly. London, Henry Frowde [1907].

Chandler, Frank W. The Literature of Roguery. 2 volumes. Boston, Houghton Mifflin Co., 1907.

————— Romances of Roguery. New York, Columbia University Press, 1899.

Chase, Lewis N. The English Heroic Play. New York, Macmillan Co., 1903.

Clarke, Samuel. Sermons on Several Subjects. London, G. and W. B. Whittaker, R. Priestley, and R. Bliss, 1820.

Collection of Miscellany Letters, A, Selected out of *Mist's Weekly Journal.* 2 volumes. London, N. Mist, 1722.

Collier, Jeremy. Miscellanies; In Five Essays . . . the Four Last by Way of Dialogue. London, Sam. Keeble . . . and Jo. Hindmarsh, 1694.

[Collins, Anthony]. A Discourse Concerning Ridicule and Irony in Writing. London, J. Brotherton, 1729.

Common Sense; or, The Englishman's Journal. . . . 2 volumes. London, J. Purser and G. Hawkins, 1738–39.

Complete Newgate Calendar . . . The. Edited by J. L. Rayner and G. T. Crook. 5 volumes. London, Navarre Society, 1926.

[Coventry, Francis]. An Essay on the New Species of Writing Founded by Mr. Fielding. . . . London, W. Owen, 1751.

—— The History of Pompey the Little; or, The Life and Adventures of a Lap-Dog [1751]. [London], The Golden Cockerel Press, 1926.

Craftsman; Being a Critique on the Times, The. London, J. Smith, 1727.

Craftsman . . . The. London, R. Francklin, 1731–38.

Crane, R. S. ["Reviews"], PQ, XI (April, 1932), 203–6.

—— "Suggestions toward the Genealogy of the 'Man of Feeling,'" ELH, I (December, 1934), 205–29.

Cross, Wilbur L. The History of Henry Fielding. 3 volumes. New Haven, Yale University Press, 1918.

Cumberland, Richard. A Treatise of the Laws of Nature [1672], Made English from the Latin by John Maxwell. London, R. Phillips [1727].

Daily Post, The. London, 1719–1746 [?].

De Castro, J. Paul. "Fieldingiana," Notes and Queries, 12 series, II (December 2, 1916), 441–43; 12 series, III (January 27, 1917), 74.

—— " 'Jonathan Wild the Great,' " Notes and Queries, 12 series, III (January 27, 1917), 74.

Defoe, Daniel. The Complete English Tradesman in Familiar Letters. London, Charles Rivington, 1775.

—— The Fortunate Mistress . . . Edited by G. H. Maynadier. Boston, C. T. Brainard Publishing Co. [1904].

—— The Fortunes and Misfortunes of the Famous Moll Flanders. Edited by G. H. Maynadier. Boston, C. T. Brainard Publishing Co. [1903].

—— The Novels and Miscellaneous Works of Daniel Defoe. [Edited by Sir Walter Scott.] Oxford, Thomas Tegg, 1840–41.

—— Novels and Miscellaneous Works of Daniel Defoe. London, G. Bell and Sons, 1912.

—— A Plan of the English Commerce. 3d edition. London, J. and J. Rivington, 1749.

—— Romances and Narratives of Daniel Defoe. Edited by George A. Aitken. 16 volumes. London, J. M. Dent, 1895.

Digeon, Aurélien. Les Romans de Fielding. Paris, Librairie Hachette, 1923.

——— Le Texte des romans de Fielding. Paris, Les Presses Universitaires de France, 1923.

Dobson, Austin. Fielding. New York, Harper & Bros. [1883].

Dottin, Paul. Daniel Defoe et ses romans. Paris, Les Presses Universitaires de France, 1924.

Draper, John W. "The Theory of the Comic in Eighteenth-Century England," *JEGP*, XXXVII (1938), 207–21.

[Dryden, John]. The Works of John Dryden. [Edited by] Sir Walter Scott and George Saintsbury. Edinburgh, William Paterson, 1887.

Dunn, Waldo H. English Biography. London, J. M. Dent and Sons, 1916.

Dying Speeches and Behaviour of the Several State Prisoners That Have Been Executed the Last 300 Years . . . The. London, J. Brotherton, 1720.

Encyclopædia of Religion and Ethics. Edited by James Hastings. New York, Charles Scribner's Sons; Edinburgh, T. and T. Clark, 1908–22.

Englishman, The; Being a Sequel to the Guardian. London, Sam. Buckley, 1714.

Fairchild, Hoxie Neale. Religious Trends in English Poetry. New York, Columbia University Press, 1939.

[Farquhar, George]. The Dramatic Works of George Farquhar. Edited by A. C. Ewald. 2 volumes. London, John C. Nimmo, 1892.

[Fénélon, François]. Adventures of Telemachus by Fenelon. Translated by Dr. John Hawkesworth; edited by O. W. Wright. Boston, Houghton Mifflin Co., 1881.

Fielding, Henry. Amelia. Edited by G. H. Maynadier. New York, The Jenson Society, 1911.

——— An Apology for the Life of Mr. T—— C——, Comedian; Being a Proper Sequel to the Apology for the Life of Mr. Colley Cibber, Comedian. . . . London, J. Mechell, 1740.

——— The Champion; Containing a Series of Papers, Humorous, Moral, Political, and Critical, to Each of Which is Added a Proper Index to the Times. London, J. Huggonson, 1741.

——— The Covent-Garden Journal. Edited by G. E. Jensen. New Haven, Yale University Press, 1915.

——— Examples of the Interposition of Providence in the Detection and Punishment of Murder . . . with an Introduction and Conclusion Both Written by Henry Fielding, Esq. London, A. Millar, 1752.

——— The History of the Life of the Late Mr. Jonathan Wild the

Great . . . with an Introduction by Wilson Follett. New York, A. A. Knopf, 1926.

—— The History of Tom Jones, a Foundling. 2 volumes. London, Macmillan & Co., Ltd., 1924.

—— The Life of Mr. Jonathan Wild the Great, a New Edition with Considerable Corrections and Additions. London, A. Millar, 1754.

—— Miscellanies by Henry Fielding, Esq. London, A. Millar, 1743.

—— Of True Greatness; An Epistle to the Right Honourable George Dodington, Esq. London, C. Corbet, 1741.

—— The Tragedy of Tragedies; or, The Life and Death of Tom Thumb the Great; with the Annotations of H. Scriblerus Secundus. . . . Edited by James T. Hillhouse. New Haven, Yale University Press, 1918.

—— The Vernoniad Done into English from the Original Greek of Homer, Lately Found at Constantinople, with Notes *in usum*. Book the First. London, Charles Corbett, 1741.

—— The Works of Henry Fielding. Edited by Leslie Stephen. London, Smith, Elder and Co., 1882.

—— The Works of Henry Fielding, Esq. Edited by James P. Browne. London, Bickers and Son, 1903.

Fischer, Henry C. Realism and Morality in English Fiction to 1750. Pittsburgh, Pennsylvania [University of Pittsburgh dissertation], 1938. [Typewritten MS.]

Foster, James R. "The Abbé Prévost and the English Novel," *PMLA*, XLII (1927), 443–64.

Frölich, Armin. Fielding's Humor in seinen Romanen. [Inaugural dissertation, Leipzig.] Leipzig, Robert Noske, 1918.

Gagey, Edmond McAdoo. Ballad Opera. New York, Columbia University Press, 1937.

Gallery of Rogues, A. Catalogue 630. London, Maggs Bros., Ltd., 1936.

[Gay, John]. Plays Written by Mr. John Gay. . . . London, W. Strahan, 1772.

—— Polly, an Opera; Being the Second Part of The Beggar's Opera. London, T. Thomson, 1728.

Gentlemen's Magazine . . . The, by Sylvanus Urban, Gent. London, I–CCCIII, 1731–1907.

Gildon, Charles. The Deist's Manual. London, H. Roper, 1705.

Glover [Richard]. London; or, The Progress of Commerce. Dublin, George Faulkner, 1739.

Gove, Philip B. The Imaginary Voyage in Prose Fiction. New York, Columbia University Press, 1941.

Graham, Walter. English Literary Periodicals. New York, Thomas Nelson and Sons, 1930.

Guardian, The. London, Messrs. Longman [n.d.].

Harper, Charles G. Half-Hours with the Highwaymen. London, Chapman and Hall, Ltd., 1908.

Häusermann, Hans W. "Aspects of Life and Thought in *Robinson Crusoe*," *RES*, XI (July and October, 1935), 299–312; 439–56.

[Head, Richard, and Francis Kirkman]. The English Rogue; Described in the Life of Meriton Latroon, a Witty Extravagant. London, Henry Marsh, 1665–74.

Heidler, Joseph B. The History, from 1700 to 1800, of English Criticism of Prose Fiction. "University of Illinois Studies in Language and Literature," Vol. XIII, No. 2. Urbana, University of Illinois Press, 1928.

Hessler, M. D. The Literary Opposition to Sir Robert Walpole, 1721–1742. Chicago [University of Chicago dissertation], 1934. [Typewritten MS.]

Historical Register for the Year 1725, The. London, C. Meere, 1725.

[Hitchin, Charles]. The Regulator; or, A Discovery of the Thieves, Thief-Takers, and Locks, alias Receivers of Stolen Goods in and about the City of London with the Thief-Takers Proclamation, by a Prisoner in Newgate. London, T. Warner, 1718.

[Hobbes, Thomas]. The English Works of Thomas Hobbes of Malmesbury. Edited by Sir William Molesworth. London, J. Bohn, 1839–45.

Homann, Wilhelm. Henry Fielding als Humorist. [Inaugural dissertation.] Marburg, N. G. Elwert, 1900.

Hübener, Gustav. "Der Kaufmann Robinson Crusoe," *Englische Studien*, LIV (1920), 367–98.

Hudson, William Henry. A Quiet Corner in a Library. Chicago, Rand McNally and Co. [1915].

Hughes, Helen Sard. "The Middle Class Reader and the English Novel," *JEGP*, XXV (1926), 362–78.

Hume, David. A Treatise of Human Nature. . . . Edited by L. A. Selby-Bigge. Oxford, Clarendon Press, 1896.

Hutcheson, Francis. An Inquiry into the Original of our Ideas of Beauty and Virtue; In Two Treatises [1725]. 4th edition. Glasgow, Robert and Andrew Foulis, 1772.

Irving, William Henry. John Gay's London; Illustrated from the Poetry of the Time. Cambridge, Harvard University Press, 1928.

Jensen, Gerard E. "Fashionable Society in Fielding's Time," *PMLA*, XXXI (1916), 79–89.

Johnson, Samuel. A Dictionary of the English Language. 2 volumes. London, J. and P. Knapton, 1755.

Jones, B. M. Henry Fielding, Novelist and Magistrate. London, George Allen and Unwin, Ltd. [1933].

Judges, A. V. [editor]. The Elizabethan Underworld. London, George Routledge and Sons, 1930.

Ker, W. P. Epic and Romance.... London, Macmillan & Co., Ltd., 1922.

Kidson, Frank. The Beggar's Opera; Its Predecessors and Successors. Cambridge, Cambridge University Press, 1922.

Kitchin, George. A Survey of Burlesque and Parody in English. Edinburgh, Oliver and Boyd, 1931.

Knapp, Andrew, and William Baldwin. The New Newgate Calendar; Being Interesting Memoirs of Notorious Characters, Who Have Been Convicted of Outrage on the Laws of England, During the Seventeenth Century; Brought Down to the Present Time.... 5 volumes. London, J. and J. Cundee [n.d.].

Krutch, Joseph Wood. Comedy and Conscience after the Restoration. New York, Columbia University Press, 1924.

Lawrence, Frederick. The Life of Henry Fielding. London, Arthur Hall, Virtue and Co., 1855.

Lee, William. Daniel Defoe; His Life and Recently Discovered Writings. 3 volumes. London, John Camden Hotten, 1869.

Le Sage, Alain-René. The Adventures of Gil Blas de Santillana. Translated by Tobias Smollett. 2 volumes. London, Henry Frowde [1907].

L'Estrange, A. G. History of English Humour. 2 volumes. London, Hurst and Blackett [1877].

Lillo, [George]. The Christian Hero; A Tragedy. London, John Gray, 1735.

—— The London Merchant ... and Fatal Curiosity. Edited by A. W. Ward. Boston, D. C. Heath and Co., 1906.

—— The Works of Mr. George Lillo. London, T. Davies, 1775.

Lind, Levi R. "Lucian and Fielding," The Classical Weekly, XXIX (January 20, 1936), 84–86.

Lives of the Most Remarkable Criminals Who Have Been Condemned and Executed for Murder, Highway Robberies, House-breaking, Street Robberies, Coining, or other Offenses; from the Year 1720 to the Year 1735. 2 volumes. London, Reeves and Turner, 1874.

London Journal, The. London, January 17, 1720—March 17, 1744.

Longaker, Mark. English Biography in the Eighteenth Century. Philadelphia, University of Pennsylvania Press, 1931.

Lovejoy, Arthur O. The Great Chain of Being. Cambridge, Harvard University Press, 1936.

Lucian's Dialogues. Translated by Howard Williams. "Bohn's Classical Library." London, George Bell and Sons, 1888.

Lupton, William. A Discourse of Murther. London, S. Keble, 1725.

Lyons, Frederick J. Jonathan Wild, Prince of Robbers. [London], M. Joseph Ltd. [1936].

Mackintosh, Sir James. Dissertation on the Progress of Ethical Philosophy. 2d edition. Edinburgh, Adam and Charles Black, 1837.

Mallet [David]. Mustapha; A Tragedy. London, A. Millar, 1739.

Mandeville [Bernard]. An Enquiry into the Causes of the Frequent Executions at Tyburn. . . . London, J. Roberts, 1725.

———— The Fable of the Bees; or, Private Vices, Publick Benefits. [Edited] by F. B. Kaye. 2 volumes. Oxford, Clarendon Press, 1924.

Marr, George S. The Periodical Essayists of the Eighteenth Century. London, James Clarke and Co., Ltd. [1923].

[Marston, John]. The Plays of John Marston. Edited by H. Harvey Wood. 3 volumes. London and Edinburgh, Oliver and Boyd, 1938.

Mason, John E. Gentlefolk in the Making. Philadelphia [University of Pennsylvania Press], 1935.

Mist's Weekly Journal. London, Nos. 1–178, May 1, 1725—September 14, 1728.

Monthly Catalogue, The. London, Nos. 1–80, March, 1723—December, 1729.

Moore, Cecil A. Humanitarianism in the Periodical Essay and Poetry, 1700–1760. Cambridge [Harvard University doctoral dissertation], 1913. [Typewritten MS.]

———— "Shaftesbury and the Ethical Poets in England, 1700–1760," PMLA, XXXI (1916), 264–325.

———— "Whig Panegyric Verse, 1700–1760," PMLA, XLI (June, 1926), 362–401.

Morgan, Charlotte E. The Rise of the Novel of Manners. . . . New York [Columbia University Press], 1911.

Morley, Sir John. Walpole, in The Works of Lord Morley, Vol. XIII. London, Macmillan & Co., Ltd., 1921.

[Morvan de Bellegarde, J. B.]. Reflexions upon Ridicule. 4th edition. 2 volumes. London, D. Midwinter, 1727.

Mossner, Ernest Campbell. Bishop Butler and the Age of Reason. New York, Macmillan Co., 1936.

Musa Pedestris, Three Centuries of Canting Songs and Slang Rhymes

(1536–1896). Collected and annotated by John S. Farmer. [No place], Privately printed, 1896.

New Memoirs of Literature [by Michael de la Roche and others]. London, Nos. 1–6, January, 1725—December, 1727.

Nicoll, Allardyce. A History of Early Eighteenth Century Drama, 1700–1750. Cambridge, Cambridge University Press, 1929.

Nolte, Fred O. The Early Middle Class Drama, 1696–1774. "Ottendorfer Memorial Series of Germanic Monographs," No. 19. Lancaster, Pa., Lancaster Press, 1935.

[Otway, Thomas]. The Works of Thomas Otway. Edited by J. C. Ghosh. 2 volumes. Oxford, Clarendon Press, 1932.

Pabisch, Marie. Picaresque Dramas of the 17th and 18th Centuries [Inaugural dissertation (Bern)]. Göttingen, W. Fr. Kaestner, 1909.

Parker's London News; or, The Impartial Intelligencer. London, 1718[?]–1733[?].

Parnell, Thomas. Poems on Several Occasions. London, H. Lintot, 1737.

Pelham, Camden [editor]. The Chronicles of Crime. London, Reeves and Turner, 1886.

[Philips, Ambrose]. The Free-Thinker. 2d edition. London, J. Brindley, 1733.

Pike, Luke Owen. A History of Crime in England. London, Smith, Elder and Co., 1876.

Plain Dealer, The, [by Aaron Hill and others]. London, Nos. 1–117, March 23, 1724—May 7, 1725.

Pleasaunt Historie of Lazarillo de Tormes, The, Drawen out of Spanish by David Rowland of Anglesey (1586). Edited by J. E. V. Crofts. "The Percy Reprints," No. 7. Oxford, Basil Blackwell, 1924.

Political State of Great Britain, The. London, J. Baker, 1712–40.

[Pope, Alexander]. The Works of Alexander Pope. [Edited] by the Rev. Whitwell Elwin and W. J. Courthope. London, John Murray, 1871–89.

Present State of the Republick of Letters, The. London, Nos. 1–18, 1728–36.

[Prévost, Antoine]. The Life and Entertaining Adventures of Mr. Cleveland. 3d edition. London, James Rivington and J. Fletcher, 1760.

——— Oeuvres choisies de l'Abbé Prévost. Amsterdam, Rue et Hôtel Serpente, 1783.

[Purney, Thomas]. The Works of Thomas Purney. Edited by H. O. White. "The Percy Reprints," No. 12. Oxford, Basil Blackwell, 1933.

[Quevedo y Villegas, Don Francisco de]. The Comical Works of Don

Francisco de Quevedo. Translated from the Spanish [by Capt. John Stevens]. 2d edition. London, J. Woodward, 1709.

—— The Visions of Dom Francisco de Quevedo Villegas . . . Made English by Sir Roger L'Estrange. 8th edition. London, Richard Sare and E. Hindmarsh, 1696.

Richards, E. A. Hudibras in the Burlesque Tradition. New York, Columbia University Press, 1937.

[Richardson, Samuel]. The Works of Samuel Richardson. 12 volumes. London, Henry Sotheran and Co., 1883.

Robbins, Alfred F. "'Jonathan Wild the Great'; Its Germ," Notes and Queries, 11 series, II (October 1, 1910), 261–63.

—— "'Jonathan Wild, the Great,'" Notes and Queries, 12 series, III (January 13, 1917), 38–39; (March 24, 1917), 237–38.

Robertson, J. M. Bolingbroke and Walpole. London, T. Fisher Unwin, Ltd. [1919].

—— A Short History of Morals. London, Watts and Co., 1920.

Rowe [Nicholas]. Tamerlane; A Tragedy. 5th edition. London, J[acob] T[onson], 1720.

[St. John, Henry]. The Works of Lord Bolingbroke. 4 volumes. Philadelphia, Carey and Hart, 1841.

Saint-Pierre [Charles Irénée Castel], Abbé de. Ouvrages de morale et de politique. [Title varies.] Rotterdam, Jean Daniel Beman, 1729–41.

Scarron, Paul. The Comical Romance, and Other Tales, Done into English by Tom Brown, John Savage, and Others, with an Introduction by J. J. Jusserand. 2 volumes. London, Lawrence and Bullen, 1892.

Schultz, William Eben. Gay's Beggar's Opera; Its Content, History, and Influence. New Haven, Yale University Press, 1923.

Scot's Magazine, The. Edinburgh, I–LXV, 1739–1803.

[Secker, Thomas]. The Works of Thomas Secker, L.L.D. . . . A New Edition. Edinburgh, James Dickson, 1792.

Shaftesbury, Anthony Ashley Cooper, Earl of. Characteristics of Men, Manners, Opinions, Times, etc. Edited by J. M. Robertson. London, Grant Richards, 1900.

Sherburn, George. "Fielding's Amelia; An Interpretation," ELH, III (March, 1936), 1–14.

Sidgwick, Henry. Outlines of the History of Ethics. London, Macmillan and Co., 1886.

Singer, Hans Wolfgang. Das bürgerliche Trauerspiel in England. Leipzig, Reudnitz, 1891.

Smith, Captain Alexander. A Complete History of the Lives and Rob-

beries of the Most Notorious Highwaymen, Footpads, Shoplifts and
Cheats of Both Sexes. Edited by Arthur L. Hayward, New York,
Brentano's, [1926].
—— The Thieves Grammar. London, Sam. Briscoe [c.1720].
Spanish Libertines, The; or, The Lives of Justina, the Country Jilt;
Celestina, the Bawd of Madrid; and Estevanillo de Gonzales, the
Most Arch and Comical of Scoundrels, to Which Is Added a Play,
Call'd An Evening's Adventures, Now First Made English by Cap-
tain John Stevens. London, Samuel Bunchley, 1707.
Spectator, The. [Edited by] George A. Aitken. 8 volumes. London, John
C. Nimmo, 1898.
Spingarn, Joel Elias. A History of Literary Criticism in the Renaissance.
New York, Published for the Columbia University Press by Macmil-
lan Co., 1899.
Stauffer, Donald A. The Art of Biography in Eighteenth Century Eng-
land. Princeton, Princeton University Press, 1941.
Steele, Richard. The Christian Hero [1701]. Dublin, George Risk, 1725.
—— The Conscious Lovers [1722]. London, John Bell, 1791.
Stephen, Leslie. English Literature and Society in the Eighteenth Cen-
tury. London, Duckworth and Co., 1904.
—— History of English Thought in the Eighteenth Century. 2 vol-
umes. London, Smith, Elder and Co., 1876.
Stevens, David Harrison. "Some Immediate Effects of *The Beggar's
Opera*," in The Manly Anniversary Studies in Language and Litera-
ture. Chicago, University of Chicago Press, 1923.
Sutherland, James R. Defoe. Philadelphia, J. B. Lippincott Co., 1938.
—— "*The Beggar's Opera*," *TLS* (April 25, 1935), p. 272.
[Swift, Jonathan]. The Poems of Jonathan Swift. Edited by Harold
Williams. Oxford, Clarendon Press, 1937.
—— The Prose Works of Jonathan Swift, D.D. Edited by Temple
Scott. London, George Bell and Sons, 1902.
Tatler, The. Edited by George A. Aitken. New York, Hadley and
Mathews, 1899.
Thomson [James]. Edward and Eleonora; A Tragedy. London, The
Author, 1739.
—— The Tragedy of Sophonisba. London, The Company, 1730.
Thorndike, Ashley H. English Comedy. New York, Macmillan Co..
1929.
Thornbury, Ethel Margaret. Henry Fielding's Theory of the Comic
Prose Epic. "University of Wisconsin Studies in Language and Liter-
ature," No. 30. Madison, University of Wisconsin, 1931.

Thurmond, John. Harlequin Sheppard; A Night Scene in Grotesque Characters. London, J. Roberts and A. Dodd, 1724.

Tieje, Arthur J. "The Expressed Aim of the Long Prose Fiction from 1579 to 1740," *JEGP*, XI (1912), 402–32.

Trent, W. P. Daniel Defoe; How to Know Him. Indianapolis, Bobbs-Merrill Co. [1916].

Turberville, A. S. English Men and Manners in the Eighteenth Century. Oxford, Clarendon Press, 1929.

Universal Journal, The. London, Nos. 1–38, December 11, 1723—August 29, 1724.

Universal Spectator and Weekly Journal, The [by Henry Baker and others]. London, October 12, 1728—March 1, 1746.

Ustick, W. L. "Changing Ideals of Aristocratic Character and Conduct in Seventeenth-Century England," *MP*, XXX (November, 1932), 147–66.

Voltaire [François Marie Arouet]. Histoire de l'empire de Russie, sous Pierre-le-Grand. Paris, Chez Treuttel et Würtz [1835].

────── The History of Charles XII, King of Sweden. Translated from the French. 6th edition. London, C. Davis, 1735.

Voorde, Frans Pieter Van der. Henry Fielding, Critic and Satirist. [Amsterdam], Pier Westerbaan, 1931.

Ward, Ned. The London Spy. Edited by Arthur L. Hayward. New York, George H. Doran Company [n.d.].

Waterland, Daniel. Sermons on Several Important Subjects. 2d edition. 2 volumes. London, S. Leacroft, 1776.

Wells, J. E. "The 'Champion' and Some Unclaimed Essays by Henry Fielding," *Englische Studien*, XLVI (1912–13), 355–66.

────── "Fielding's 'Champion' and Captain Hercules Vinegar," *MLR*, VIII (1913), 165–72.

────── "Fielding's Political Purpose in *Jonathan Wild*," *PMLA*, XXVIII (1913), 1–55.

────── "News for Bibliophiles," *The Nation*, XCVI (January 16, 1913), 53–54.

Whewell, William. Lectures on the History of Moral Philosophy in England. London, John W. Parker and Son, 1852.

White, H. O. "Thomas Purney . . ." Essays and Studies of the English Association, Vol. XV. Oxford, Clarendon Press, 1929.

Whitehall Evening Post, The. London, Nos. 1–3330, 1718—June 24, 1738.

Whitney, Lois. Primitivism and the Idea of Progress in English Popular

Literature of the Eighteenth Century. Baltimore, Johns Hopkins Press, 1934.

Whittuck, Charles. The "Good Man" of the XVIIIth Century. London, George Allen, 1901.

Williams, Basil. The Whig Supremacy, 1714–1760. Vol. XI, Oxford History of England; edited by G. N. Clark. Oxford, Clarendon Press, 1939.

Wollaston [William]. The Religion of Nature Delineated. 8th edition. London, J. Beecroft, 1759.

Works of the English Poets, The. Edited by Alexander Chalmers. London, J. Johnson, 1810.

Wright, Louis B. Middle-Class Culture in Elizabethan England. Chapel Hill, University of North Carolina Press, 1935.

[Young, Edward]. The Complete Works of the Rev. Edward Young, L.L.D. . . . 2 volumes. London, William Tegg and Co., 1854.

INDEX